Vermont

Trout Hikes

A Guide to its Backwoods Ponds

Peter Shea

Jack, You don't have to fish to enjoy these places. "Peter"

Back cover photograph of author: Clem Nilan

Front cover photograph of Pleiad Lake, as well as all other photos and maps, are by the author.

First Edition
Printed in the United States of America

ISBN: 978-0-578-76640-9

Other Books by Peter Shea

Vermont Trout Ponds: A Personal Selection, Commentary, and True Stories

Long Trail Trout: Backcountry Fly-Fishing Adventures, from Vermont to Montana, and Beyond

Vermont's Trophy Trout Waters: An Atlas & Guide

Collateral Trout: A Vermonter's Angling Memoirs and Fishy Tales

The New Atlas of Vermont Trout Ponds: A GPS-Compatible Guidebook

Vermont Trout Streams: A Fly Angler's Guide to the Best (with co-author Bob Shannon)

Acknowledgments

I want to express my appreciation to the several Vermont fisheries biologists, who took time to review the extent and intentions of this book. I have come to them so many times in the past, yet each time they respond amid their overly busy schedules, and where appropriate add their useful suggestions, or share their information. My appreciation extends to Vermont's fisheries biologists Joel Flewelling, Dave Gibson, Shawn Good, Bret Ladago, Bernie Pientka, Lee Simard, and Lael Will.

In the realm of backwoods trout, Vermont's Northeast Kingdom is a region that has been particularly favored by the trout gods. As a result, the burden and breadth of help that I received from the two fisheries biologists who work this beat was considerable. Given this, I am particularly indebted to Pete Emerson and Jud Kratzer. Every day, like their cohorts above, they bring their knowledge and commitment to Vermont's fishery, to its great benefit.

Finally, I thank my dear wife, Carol, for her help, design suggestions, and proofreading; and, to my friend Steve Alexander for his cover design.

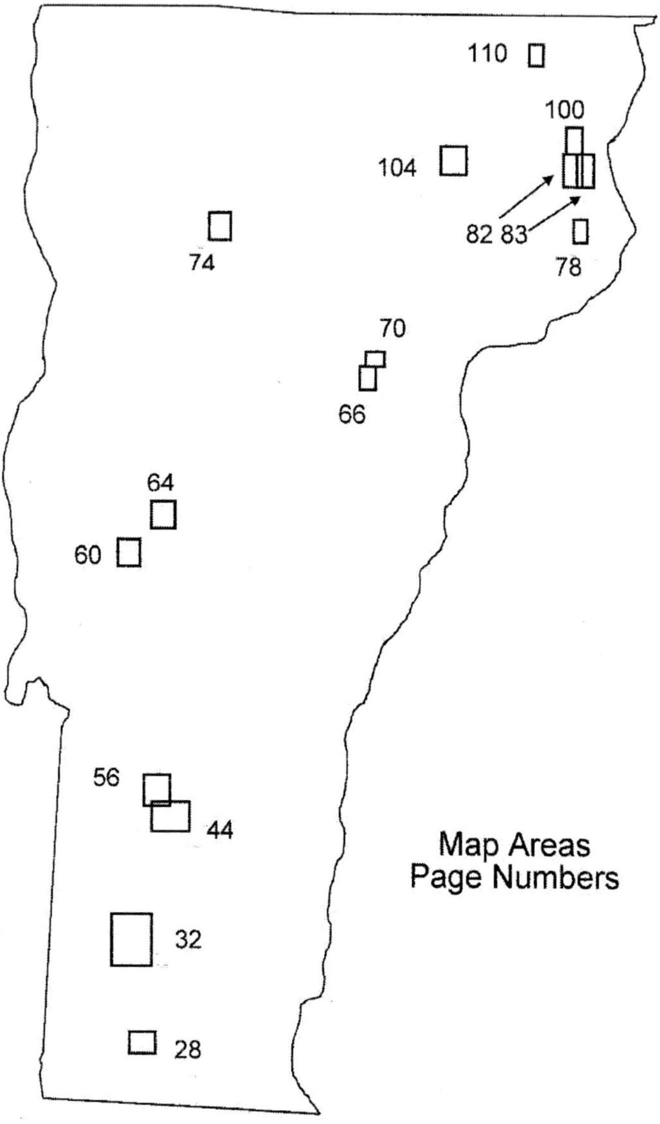
110
100
104
82 83
74
78
70
66
64
60
56
44
Map Areas
Page Numbers
32
28

Introduction

A Personal Word

An arguably apocryphal story: Willy Sutton, a famous bank robber of nearly a century ago, was once asked why he robbed banks. His reply was cogent: "Because that's where the money is."

Although this guidebook includes information on a few streams, it is only because they are in such very close proximity to the ponds addressed here, it would be wrong not to include them, as well. They also offer great angling prospects. The focus here, however, reflects my longtime personal interest in Vermont's trout ponds, and, referring to Willy's commitment, it's because that's where the big *brook* trout are.

But, why a *guide* to these backwoods waters?

It comes down to the simple thing of trying to share my passion for these special Vermont places, and in so doing, encourage some attention to their preservation and husbandry. There just aren't that many.

The reason that diamonds, Picassos, and the dilithium crystals that powered the starship Enterprise have such high value is their rarity. So it is with Vermont's "backwoods" trout ponds. For purposes of this book, they are defined as those that require an angler *to hike* to get to them, even if it's only a short portage of a few hundred feet.

By my estimate there are now fewer than two dozen of these places in the state. I have fished nearly all of these, including some additional ones that no longer hold trout. The selection included here is purely a personal one.

I am crazy for fishing these places, and have fished them for the last fifty years. The kind of magic they hold for me is perhaps conveyed a little by recalling a trip to a certain reclusive pond in southern Vermont. It was the Columbus Day weekend, the solemn high holiday of the fall foliage *haj,* when thousands of tourists, including hikers and anglers, come to visit our state.

That evening's outing had yielded two very special, eight-inch brook trout. They were what I call "football trout," with shapes more like bass. They were hunch-shouldered, with jaws kiped, as you might expect to see on a 15-inch brookie. Adorned with a riot of spawning colors, their bellies matched the fiery trees of October, and the scarlet constellation points on their flanks were surrounded by a royal blue that would shame a bird of paradise. There are many larger brookies, and other large trout, that have long faded from memory, but this prized brace will always be vividly recalled.

The only other person sharing this pond during my stay was my backpacking partner. In the glare of brilliant morning sunshine, he had managed to sleep in, while a pack of coyotes came whooping, yelling and howling, within thirty feet of where we were camped, before they veered off in a panicked surprise.

We hiked out later on that glorious autumn day. In the midst of Vermont's busiest tourist season, we had just spent three entire days without seeing another soul. This was true even on the trailed portion of our hike. There are wild places in Wyoming or Montana where you cannot easily accomplish this.

Some of the ponds noted here host wild brook trout well beyond a foot in length. But their value and meaning are way beyond the fish. These backwoods waters are places to see an eagle steal a trout from an osprey; to be transfixed by a *field* of lady slippers; to get nervous as you confront a moose; to listen to an otter crunch on the bones of a living fish; to have a hummingbird perch on a cord that guys your tent; and, to fall asleep to the tremolos of the loon and the splashes of feeding trout.

Until I was in my mid-twenties, the idea of fishing for trout in a pond was not at all on my radar. Like all prejudices, it was passed on. Considering that my father went to work all his life in a t-shirt and Dickies pants from Woolworth's, he had a rather patrician view of this kind of fishing. According to him it was a place to angle for coarse fish with a forked stick, and this was not our game.

I was introduced to the idea of catching some trout *in a pond,* about fifty years ago, by a certain lawbreaking resident of St. Johnsbury whom I was counseling at the time, and who kindly provided me detailed directions to a pond, along with the promise of truly wild brookies.

In the course of a couple of seasons, I made three or four trips into this pond without luck. I didn't know much. Daytime fly fishing in August is not the most effective strategy and tactic. During much of these dog days, many of Vermont's ponds are in a severe temperature lock. In shallow ponds the trout are schooled up around springs, or have scooted up feeder streams. In deeper ponds the thermocline, and cooler water, may be ten or fifteen feet down, and *as usual* I was fishing either right on top, or in the top two feet of water. I mostly still do.

Eventually I caught on to my folly. Spring, early summer, and the fall became my favored times to fish these places. I am not sure how I became captivated with these waterbodies, but I have developed a proclivity for these still water fisheries to the detriment of the time spent stream fishing. No real regrets there, as this siren call has brought me to some of North America's wildest places, as well as more than a score of these Vermont hike-in treasures, the best of which are included here.

There is a mystery to the waters of a lake or a pond. A stream or river presents the trained eye some obvious places where trout can lurk. A lake or a pond, at least at initial observation, even for trained eyes, often offers up a blank slate. Given a decent temperature range, even a tough day on a stream will likely yield at least a little stinker or two. A pond or a lake will do you no favors like that. The fish can "disappear" for days on end.

On the other hand, that still water can explode into action, with fish of eye-popping size, jumping all over the place, making your knees weak and your hands shake with excitement.

Even the lone dimple, made by a small brookie in still water, can take on distorted proportions, as its wake laps against you, travelling a hundred feet or more from its mysterious source. Whether it's a match to reality or not, your mind's eye sees that fish as a lunker, and your heart races to this fish's rise as it did when you were ten years old.

The Maps and Depth Charts

The maps in this book are intended to supplement and illustrate the access descriptions provided in the text.

Road networks are not completely illustrated, nor are the stream networks, so they are not at all useful for travel that is extraneous to the routes and places described in the text. For nearly all of the ponds included, there are additional trails and roads that will get you there. My editorial decisions were directed by a variety of factors. Perhaps it was the better road, or easier to hike, or maybe a route that offers the best angling options, or just a way that provides the most clarity in getting there.

Please note that the **abbreviations** for the Long Trail and Appalachian Trail are LT and AT, respectively, or, where they coincide, are abbreviated LT/AT; Forest Service Roads are labeled "F.S.R."

The depth charts are reinterpretations of the Department of Environmental Conservation charts, or hand sketched soundings of Vermont's fisheries biologists and water resource personnel. They are included to help you develop fishing strategies, not for purposes of "navigation." Navigation hazards are not shown, and there are submerged rocks out there, ready to tip a laden canoe. Perhaps the idea of a depth chart of a waterbody that is only five or six feet deep seems a little absurd. For sure, I debated its merits. In the end I thought that if the deepest part of a pond is only five feet deep, I'd want to know where that is.

Getting There and *Getting Back*

Arranged from south to north, more or less, all of the ponds cited in this guidebook can be accessed by the simple road and hiking directions provided. The GPS coordinates provided in the headings, denote either the location of the pond, or some explicitly stated place that is specified in the text.

In some cases, I have added GPS coordinates to clarify and assist in the directions. You can just punch these in to whatever digital map that you are using on your phone, or into any handheld GPS instrument that you are using. These GPS references are used more often in Vermont's northeast region. Here, there is a network of logging roads that are not always well marked, and even when marked can be confusing. How do you deal with an intersection from which three roads depart, all with the same name? Or, how do you effectively drive a stretch of road that in the course of a few miles has three separate roads, entering both from the left and the right, and all of these roads have the same name of the road you are travelling?

Seasoned backcountry travelers can probably take a pass on reading the remainder of what follows under this heading. No doubt it will sound a little preachy, but I'll risk that against the fact that you, the reader, might be new to hiking and backpacking.

Backpacking or hike-in anglers are in a small minority. Welcome to the club. Although you won't need a map and compass to get you to the ponds included here, it's a good idea to know their use, first and foremost for safety but also to explore areas that have no trails, and that lie adjacent to the destinations addressed here.

It was several years ago that the Burlington media was reporting that a lost middle-aged man was successfully found after a two-day search. For me, the interesting part of this hunter's story was his quote: "I was using a compass and a handheld GPS, and they were wrong."

Wrong? No. I could pretty much guess at what had happened, and that his compass and GPS tools were each functioning perfectly. They just weren't talking to each other properly.

Nearly all GPS devices leave the factory at the default setting of "true north," i.e. they are set to the North Pole. A compass points to "magnetic north," currently a point on the earth about 500 miles northwest of Baffin Bay in Canada, where a concentration of iron, deep within the earth, attracts the points of our compass needles. This place is about 900 miles from the real North Pole, so this difference can cause confusion when you use a compass.

Topographic maps, and now other online sources, provide a critical piece of information for any point on the planet: magnetic declination. This is the measure (in degrees) that true north is separated from magnetic north, and if you are using a compass, you must account for it when you are hiking to your destination. Our lost hunter was no doubt unknowingly using the conflicting systems in his travel, and the farther you walk a bearing (a specific direction) the more that mistake will start to matter.

Let me rough this out. Let's say you are in Vermont's Northeast Kingdom. In general terms, the magnetic declinations in this region are about 15 degrees. Let's say your destination, a little pond with fat brookies, is directly north of you, i.e. your map bearing is 0° or 360°. (They're the same. Both are "due north.") Let's say it's a two-mile hike, through unbroken forest. If you do not account for that 15-degree declination, you'll be in trouble. After accurately walking that bearing due north, for two miles, you will miss that pond, passing west of it by a full half-mile. That's what a 15-degree error will do.

Here is my point. If you are going to hike to some of the ponds in this book, especially the few that are trailless, you should have a working knowledge of maps, compasses, and GPS technicalities. The maps I have drawn are only intended to illustrate the written directions, and not intended for navigation.

Learn to navigate with a map and compass. The skills involved are easy to learn, and come in real handy when the batteries go dead, when the forest canopy blocks out the satellite signals, or where phone reception is unavailable.

Let me recommend a book that I encountered as a pre-teen, and led me to many trout fishing adventures. Bjorn Kjellstrom's Be Expert with Map & Compass has been in print for nearly seventy years, and offers a very clear instructional guide to the subject. Then, get a topographic map of the area you are visiting, and practice what you learned. The skills you acquire will allow you to explore the trailless areas around the ponds cited here. You may find great fishing in a virginal beaver dam, or gain an amazing vista from some lonely part of the Green Mountain State.

Camping

"...and at the bottom of the cliff was another pile of garbage. And we decided that one big pile was better than two little piles, and rather than bring that one up, we decided to throw ours down. That's what we did."

Arlo Guthrie
"Alice's Restaurant"

No, my song reference above does not lead to an admonition about littering and employing no-trace camping. Those behaviors are just stipulated: they are a given. Instead, for me there is convoluted analogy to be found in those song lines. It runs through my mind whenever I chance upon a well-established social campsite that is out of compliance with the local requirements for camping. The thing is, *they are all out of compliance!* This is true because virtually every one of these backcountry, rogue campsites is set too close to the water. The backpacker is faced with a sort of similar quandary as the young Guthrie faced.

One solution is to use the established campsite just as a hangout spot. Sleep, prepare meals (on a stove), wash dishes, and go Number Two, at a healthy 200-plus feet distance from the water's edge. (On the Internet, there are scores of videos that demonstrate recommended methods for how to poop in the woods.) If you insist on sleeping in the established campsite, you should conduct all other business, as above, and, as temping as that fire-ring may be, forgo the campfire, as well.[1]

---

[1] There are benefits to not having a campfire. For one, you have more time to fish, instead of running around collecting downed wood. You may also see more wildlife, because you are not broadcasting your presence for miles, nor is there smoke odor on your person.

Depending on where you are there are different requirements but there are some basic principles that you should observe everywhere; even within designated **National Wilderness** areas visitors should:

- Plan ahead and prepare
- Travel and camp on durable surfaces
- Dispose of waste properly
- Leave what you find and take home what you brought
- Minimize campfire impacts
- Respect wildlife
- Be considerate of other visitors

Once outside of a designated wilderness area, there are a number of governing entities that hold sway on the regulations related to backcountry camping. Within the area of a **National Forest**, the following is recommended: Locate campsites at least 200′ from trails or waterbodies. When able, utilize sites already managed for overnight use, including tent platforms and established shelters. To protect fragile areas, do not camp in alpine or sub-alpine areas where trees are eight feet high or less.

Vermont State Forests allow primitive camping, within designated areas of selected state lands, with these provisos:

- Camping must be at least 100 feet from any stream or body of water

- Camping must be at least 200 feet from any trail or property line, and 1,000 feet from any traveled road.
- Camping allowed up to three consecutive nights.
- Groups of 11 or more must obtain a permit from the District Office in order to primitive camp.
- Only dead/down trees/branches may be used for firewood.
- Camping above 2,500 feet in elevation is prohibited unless otherwise designated.
- There must be one responsible adult for every four campers under the age of 14.
- If you carry it in – carry it out!
- Leave your campsite so clean that no one else can find it.
- The use of backpacker stoves with self-contained fuel is urged.

Finally, certain Vermont Fish and Wildlife's **Wildlife Management Areas** permit primitive camping for the purpose of fishing, hunting, or trapping. F&W limits the stay to three days, and defines it, "as occupying a site in a natural environment with no developed facilities, leaving the site in its original condition so there is no or minimal evidence of human visitation." In addition, the campsites must be at least 200 feet from any waterbody, property line, or road within the Wildlife Management Area.

There are numerous online sources to educate you to the details of no-trace travel and camping. At the minimum, you should learn the protocols for cooking, food storage and disposal, and perhaps most importantly latrine practices. We have all come upon disaster zones by the sides of wooded highways. No one wants to see one in these reclusive places. There are a plethora of YouTube videos that describe a variety of "best practices."

Several of the ponds in this book are on or adjacent to Vermont's 270-mile long "Long Trail." This is North America's oldest long distance hiking trail,[2] and was the inspiration for what became the Appalachian Trail. The two trails actually coincide for almost a hundred miles, starting from the Massachusetts State line to Killington, Vermont.

The Green Mountain Club has been the creative agency and protector of the trail for more than a hundred years. Membership offers access to discounts at shelters, as well as a wealth of guide information on the Long Trail, and the hundreds of miles of trail that the Club maintains. See: www.greenmountainclub.org.

---

[2] Native Americans did not "hike."

A Word on Fishing a Pond with a Fly

Strategies for finding fish in these ponds are the same as for any lake or pond: looking for the inlets and outlets, seeking out the seepage of cold springs at the edges, as well as for "shelves" where the depths drop off rapidly. At the edge of a bed of lily pads is one of my favorites – or knock it up to 3X tippet, and go *into* the pads with a dry.

Think about favoring the western edge of the waterbody, late in the day. Here the "local sunset," provided by the shade of the forest's edge, may anticipate the real sunset by hours. Or, try the pond's east edge in the morning, where the sun is held at bay until it clears the trees, well after its official sunrise.

Has there been a steady wind? If so, one side of a pond may see some surface feed stacking up. "Foam lines" can also occur on still water, as well as in a river or stream, and these are always worth a going over, if you can get to them.

There are easier angling choices than opting for backwoods ponds, and that applies to the challenges you face, even after you have humped and sweated your way into one. Vermont's backwoods ponds are usually ringed by forest cover, and where there are open areas, they are most likely created by bogs and other wetland.

If you are fishing with a spinning rod, either with lures or bait, you just need a place to stretch your arms out from the forest cover, and you're pretty much in business. Fishing with a fly, however, you face real problems with casting.

Within the covers of this book you will find a few ponds that are a short enough hike to allow you to haul in a canoe, kayak, or lightweight jon-boat. Casting problem solved. (Check the regs on the use of gasoline power.)

The next best is using a float tube. If you never have packed and used one, you need to consider the commitment involved in carrying it, and all the accoutrement that is required. Although lighter than a canoe or other watercraft, you will be adding plenty of weight to that pack. Whether you are day-hiking or backpacking for an overnight stay, you will be adding about twenty pounds to your carry.

Here are some ballpark estimates of the additional load related to a float tube:

1) the float tube itself, 15 lbs.
2) swim fins for propulsion, 4 lbs.
3) in cold water, add a pair of fly-weight stocking-foot waders, another 2-3 lbs.
4) the luxury of a pump with hose, 1 lb. or more
5) lightweight sandals and heavy or neoprene socks (unless you want to bring along your hiking

boots for the float. You will need these to walk back to camp or the trail, if your tube is ever blown to the other side of the lake, 1 lb. Personally, I get really nervous when I think about bringing my hiking boots out on a float.

6) an anchor rope and a stout mesh bag to fill with a few rocks for an anchor; call it 1 lb.
7) Vermont requires a U.S. Coast Guard-approved life jacket – perhaps another 1 lb.[3]

Take a pass on those options above, then you will be fishing like I have for the overwhelming majority of my backwoods trips, i.e. either staying dry-foot on shore with hiking boots, or wading. Doing the latter, in the early spring or late in the fall, I use featherweight stocking-foot waders, and the lightest wading shoes I can get hold of. Once the water warms up (out of the fifties, at least) you can wade wet, for a while, if you've got something dry to change into when the sun goes down.

I've used lightweight, strap-on on sandals, and ripstop nylon pants – essentially "pajama bottoms" that I sewed myself. I tuck the pants into the neoprene socks. You need socks and pants (or waders) to keep the leeches off you. They absolutely abound in most of these ponds.

---

[3] A backpacker can arrange the classic three-panel life jacket, so that it forms a sleeping pad, perhaps a little short, but nearly comparable to the closed-cell foam pads in use. It's not a Therm-a-Rest, but it will serve.

The footwear has to be super secure, or you'll leave them in the mud. Wading can get you a lot more casting real estate, but in some cases you may only get out two or three feet.

Fishing these places with a fly, and keeping a dry foot, is a real challenge. A long roll-cast is a real asset that I've yet to master, so I've relied on ferreting out those few locations that offer a little room for an upward angled backcast, or some longer side-casting. Ponds that have irregular shorelines will present places where they "turn a corner." Placing yourself at the apex of this "turn" will give you a chance to side-cast into deeper water on either side. Bear in mind, however, that the ten feet of water from the shoreline out, can be some of the best places to find lurking trout, no matter what its depth. (Many times, isn't this the water you are fishing when you are in a boat?)

Some ponds offer an occasional rock outcrop as a casting perch. A little pair of binoculars will help you scout a pond's perimeter. The low brush opening of an adjoining wetland, or a bog, can allow for a high thrown backcast. Often you can find dry footing – or near-dry footing on some hummocks within the wetland. You can also pick an edge of this opening that is suited to your right- or left-hand cast. When I was spry and careless, walking out on fallen trees seemed like a good idea.

However, best of all is being blessed by the trout gods and the kindness of strangers! There is a wonderful Vermont custom that you may encounter: the "social boat." These are boats left for use by pond visitors that you will find at some lakes. They may be pulled on shore near the trail, or squirreled away nearby. They may or may not have oars. Hopefully they are watertight. I have used some that require you spend equal time between bailing and casting. The rule of their use is simple: *return the craft to where you found it.* Even if you're in a "social boat," the State of Vermont demands that you have a life jacket as well. Please note: social boats are not found on the properties of lakeside camps. Leave these alone.

Some Flies

My angling forte, if any at all, has always been where-to, not how-to, so I will make only some limited recommendations as to flies.

Let's start at the very top of "must-haves." In late June through early August, you should have a ready supply of "hex" (*hexagenia limbata*) in your tackle box. These are large (#10 - #6) light colored mayflies, most often with greenish or cream bodies and a dark cream to white wing. There are also darker versions, about 80% of the size of the light hex. I've seen these earlier in the calendar.

The nymphs can live for up to a couple of years, burrowing in the mud and getting BIG. The result is that when this hatch is on, large trout will forgo their usual predilection for smaller fish, and come out and play.

I have developed my own pattern for these, sometimes using 4X long hooks. I tie a forked-tail, and an oversized squirrel- or calf-tail wing with a parachute hackle. These little catamaran-like sailboats are very effective, but I had fished pretty successfully for years using #10 Muddler Minnows to imitate hex.

A forked-tail hex pattern viewed from above

You should also always have a very large version of a Cinnamon Ant, #8s or #10s. When the winged versions of these large ants land in numbers on a pond, there is as least as much mayhem as there is for the hex – maybe more. They are rare and irregular, but when this dance is playing, you don't want to be a wallflower.

One of the early spring hatches is a fly matched nicely by using Slate-Winged Mahoganies in sizes #12-#14. Other good flies are Leeches, Black and Gray Ghosts, caddis in all colors and sizes, as well as Wooly Buggers in all sizes and colors.

In the early fall, Blue-Winged Olives (#16-#20) will serve to meet the trout's interest in smaller flies. Once the spawn is on, however, it's a game of find them, and then piss them off with just about anything you throw. Big attractors work well. Have fun.

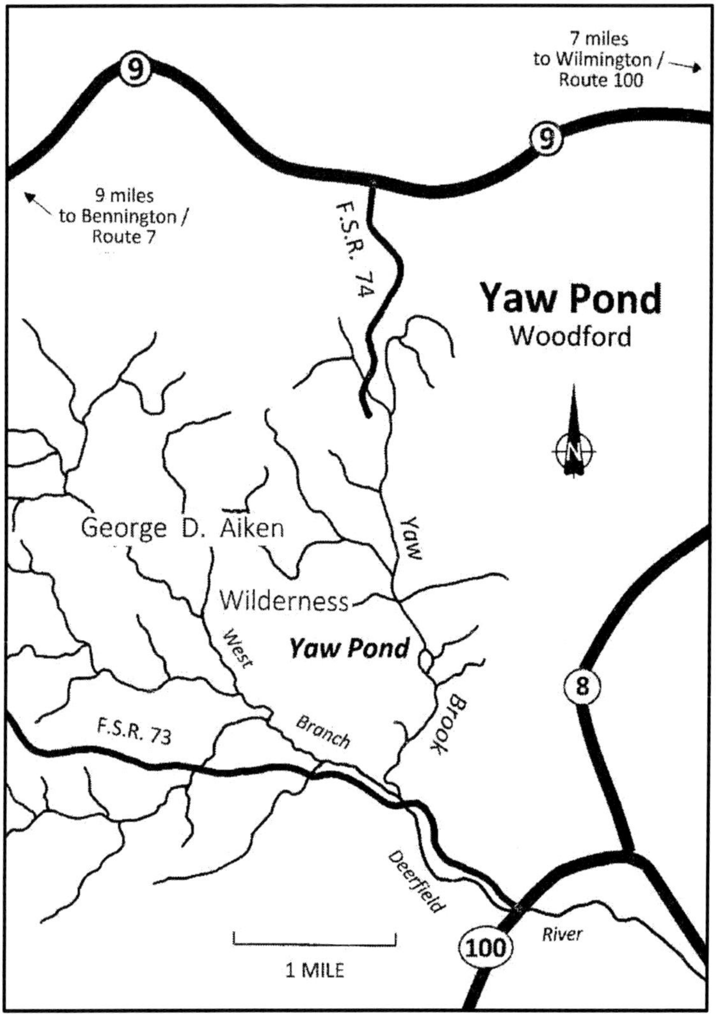
7 miles
to Wilmington /
Route 100
9
9
9 miles
to Bennington /
Route 7
F.S.R. 74
Yaw Pond
Woodford
N
George D. Aiken
Wilderness
Yaw
Yaw Pond
West
Branch
Brook
F.S.R. 73
8
Deerfield
River
100
1 MILE

Yaw Pond, N 42.8480 W 73.0129

Yaw Pond is a shallow 2-acre pond located in the town of Woodford. Its elevation is 2,014 feet. This is the jumping off point to what is arguably the wildest and wooliest trout fishing in the state. The pond lies at the southeast edge of the George D. Aiken Wilderness. This parcel is a nearly five-thousand-acre, trailless expanse of low hills, with a dendritic lattice work of small brooks and streams. It has more beaver ponds than any single angler could possibly sample. These are the headwaters of the West Branch of the Deerfield River.

It's all brook trout and all wild. And, it's all rough getting around. The walking is wet, and when the fishing is best in the spring, there are hordes of mosquitos and blackflies eager to have at you. With nothing for trails but random strips of deteriorating logging roads, a map, compass, and a knowledge of their use are requisite.

The southern route into this pond comes out of Heartwellville, but there are parking issues along the dirt road. It is, however, easily accessed from the north. Here, the George Aiken Wilderness Road (Forest Service Road #74) heads south from State Route 9, about a half mile east of Red Mill Pond. Forest Service Road 74 dead-ends in a parking area, before you hit the two-mile mark.

From here, one can follow Yaw Pond Brook downstream to a very small, but dry and level, social campsite on the left bank of the brook, just as it enters Yaw Pond. The pond lies 1.5 miles to the south of the parking area, call it 1.8 "brook-miles." The GPS coordinates in the heading mark the campsite's location.

This wilderness was named after the late Vermont senator George D. Aiken. He was a strong advocate of preservation and a leader in securing the Eastern Wilderness Act of 1975. The Aiken Wilderness is situated on a plateau rising as high as 2,300 feet.

From U.S.D.A. Forest Service website

Wilderness sight: an otter munches on a brook trout

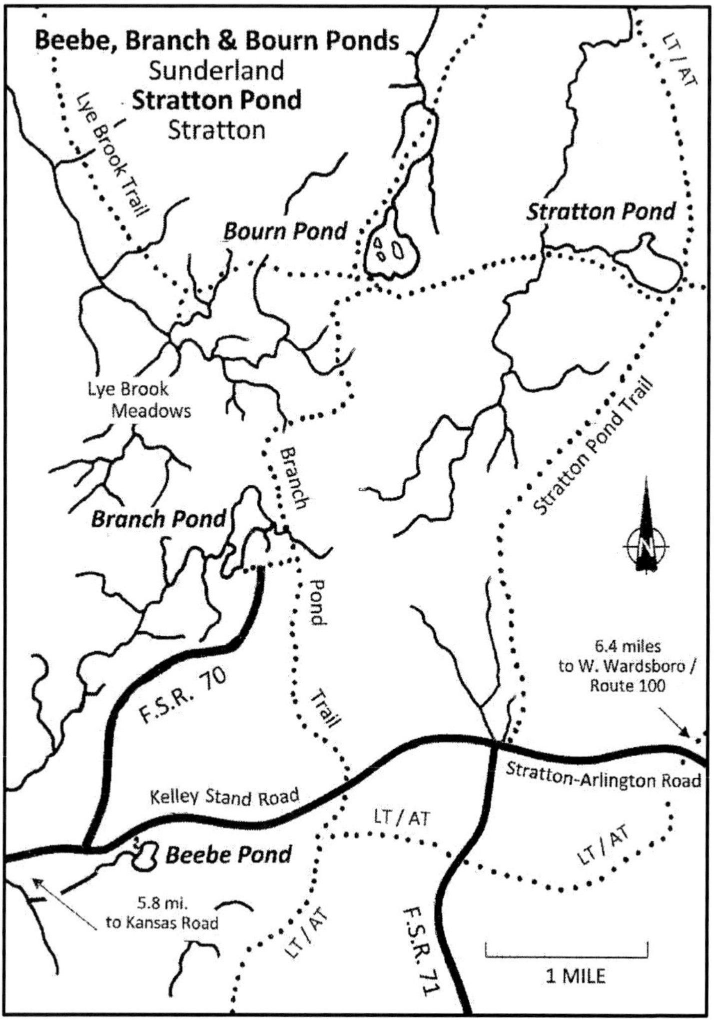
Beebe, Branch & Bourn Ponds
Sunderland
Stratton Pond
Stratton
Lye Brook Trail
LT / AT
Bourn Pond
Stratton Pond
Lye Brook
Meadows
Branch
Stratton Pond Trail
Branch Pond
Pond
6.4 miles
to W. Wardsboro /
Route 100
F.S.R. 70
Trail
Stratton-Arlington Road
Kelley Stand Road
LT / AT
LT / AT
Beebe Pond
5.8 mi.
to Kansas Road
LT / AT
F.S.R. 71
1 MILE

Beebe, Branch, Bourn, and Stratton Ponds

All of these ponds are in the Green Mountain National Forest, and most are within or bordering the Lye Brook Wilderness. They are all most easily accessed from the Kelly Stand Road in the town of Sunderland, a seasonally maintained road that is closed during the winter months. "Winter months" can sometimes include both edges of the trout season calendar.

Forest Service Road #70 is a key access point, so the directions given to its location will help you locate the trailheads of all four waterbodies.

Coming from the west side of the Green Mountains, you can use Exit 3 on Route 7. Take Route 313 west to where South Road comes in on your right. Take South Road north a short distance where it connects with the Kansas Road from East Arlington. Take the Kansas Road east (right) crossing U.S. Route 7. Continue beyond this intersection a third of a mile more, where the Kelley Stand Road comes in on the right. Take the Kelley Stand Road east six and a half miles, where you will meet the Branch Pond Road (Forest Service Road #70) on your left. It is marked by a sign that reads "Branch/Bourn Ponds Access Road."

Coming from the east side of the Green Mountains, leave State Route 100 in West Wardsboro, and head west on the Stratton-Arlington Road about 11 miles. At around the 9-mile mark, the road changes its name to the Kelly Stand Road. Just continue on this road until you meet Branch Pond Road (Forest Service Road #70,) which comes into the road from the north (on your right.)

Beebe Pond, N 43.0540 W 73.0324

Beebe Pond is an 8-acre pond in the town of Sunderland. It is located in the Green Mountain National Forest, at an elevation of 2,375 feet. Its maximum depth is 34 feet. There is easy access on a short trail. The pond has received an annual stocking of 500 to 1,000 brook trout. In the last few years the range has been 600-800. These are nice brookies by anyone's standards, running 9.6 to 9.8 inches in size.

The trailhead to Beebe Pond is nearly impossible to see from a moving car, as the trail sign is fifteen or twenty feet into the woods. Look for an innocuous looking pull-off on the south side of the Kelly Stand Road, about 0.4 miles east of Forest Service Road #70. There is room to park a couple of pickups. The trailhead coordinates are N 43.0549 W 73.0332. The narrow foot trail offers a five-minute walk, ending at a socially-established campsite, near the pond's edge.

Branch Pond, N 43.0776 W 73.0197

At an elevation of 2,637 feet, Branch Pond is among the highest in the state. It is located in Sunderland. It has a maximum depth of 34 feet, and covers 53 acres. Branch receives an occasional planting of spring fry brook trout, and an annual stocking of one-year-olds. These have numbered between 1,000 and 2,000 for the last three years. These have been very nice, 9-inch-plus brook trout.

This backwoods pond lies just outside the Lye Brook Wilderness. To access the pond take Forest Service Road #70 (Branch/Bourn Ponds Access Road,) 2.5 miles north to the Branch Pond Parking Lot. The short trail to Branch Pond is on the west side of the parking lot, and runs 600 feet to the lake, dropping downhill about fifty feet in elevation.

The boat access is undeveloped and only appropriate for a canoe or other craft that can be carried. The GPS coordinates above mark the end of the short trail from the Branch Pond parking lot.

The pond has several primitive, social campsites along its shoreline. All are handily reached from the water. On foot, there are three campsites that are easily reached from the vicinity of the boat access. At about a hundred feet or so, before you reach the launch area, a narrow foot trail enters the main trail from the right. Take this trail, which after a hundred feet or so braids relentlessly through the woods, paralleling the east shore. In the course of about 800 feet, it passes through three socially-established campsites. After that, the trail gets pretty squirrely to follow.

View of canoe/kayak launch at Branch Pond

If you are looking for a more reclusive camp, but lack a boat, another campsite is a three-quarter-mile hike. From the parking lot, take the short spur trail east, to where it joins the Branch Pond Trail. Take this trail north (left) about a third of a mile. Another short spur trail comes in from the left, and leads to a primitive campsite just above the lake shore.

Bourn Pond, N 43.1034 W 73.0032

Bourn Pond is a 55-acre pond in the town of Sunderland. It lies within the Lye Brook Wilderness, at an elevation of 2,552 feet. Its maximum depth is 26 feet. Bourn has held a decades-long reputation for producing some of the largest brook trout in the state. It is more than reputation, as U.S.F.S. samplings have kicked up brookies up to 18 inches in length. Natural reproduction is limited, however, so each year about 8,000 spring fingerling brookies are stocked, and evidently do quite well. Its most recent stocking was 9,300 so we should see a nice cohort of big trout in coming years.

The best route into Bourn is from the Branch Pond Parking Lot, reached by taking Forest Service Road #70, 2.5-miles, north from the Kelly Stand Road.

The way to Bourn Pond starts on the east side of the parking lot, and follows a short spur trail that soon joins the Branch Pond Trail, which you take north. It is about a 2.5-mile hike from the trailhead to the pond.

There are big brookies and fine scenery at Bourn Pond

The trail is easy with just some rolling ups and downs, and a net loss of elevation of about 120 feet. A common camping area is near the northwest side of the pond, which adds another three-quarters of a mile to the hike. The GPS coordinates approximately mark where the trail meets the pond from the south.

Stratton Pond, N 43.1015 W 72.9646

Stratton Pond's 46 acres sit at a 2,575-foot elevation. It has a maximum depth of 15 feet. Although Stratton Pond does not share the same reputation as Bourn Pond for big trout, I suspect that it may be simply a function of being fished less. Most of the Long Trail/Appalachian Trail thru-hikers seem to have little interest in fishing, while for the locals it's almost four miles of hiking versus the 2.5 for Bourn.

In most years from 7,000 to 9,300 brook trout fry have been planted. In the previous three years, an average of 7,500 brook trout fry have been dumped in.

With a size that is comparable to Bourn Pond, there is no reason to believe that Stratton would hold smaller fish.

The pond is located a couple of thousand feet east of the Lye Brook Wilderness boundary, right along the Long Trail/Appalachian Trail. The Green Mountain Club describes the shelter here as the busiest one on the Long Trail. Spots in the shelter and tent sites fill up by early evening. Here, I will point out a favorable difference between us anglers and the thru-hiking denizens of these monumental trails. We anglers tend to arrive much earlier at our destinations, and are quite content at pitching our tent, or dropping a pack in a shelter, at 11 in the morning, and then fish the afternoon. Or, more importantly, we want to be all set up and ready to go at the "golden hours," from say, six in the evening until you can't see any longer. So we land earlier than many of the hikers, who are always trying to add miles to their day. Early the next morning, we are fishing while the rest of the trail world is eating a hasty breakfast and packing up to go. Talk about symbiosis!

For the angler the easiest way into Stratton Pond is a mild 3.7 mile hike, using the Stratton Pond Trail. There are multiple puncheons across wet sections of trail, and they are deadly slippery when wet. The trailhead is on the Kelly Stand Road.

Coming from the east side of the Green Mountains, in West Wardsboro, and following the Stratton-Arlington Road, Forest Service Road #71 comes in from the south (left) at around the eight-mile mark. The parking lot for the Stratton Pond Trail is just east of this juncture, on the north side (the opposite side) of the road.

Coming from the west, the Stratton Pond Trail and parking are three miles east of Forest Service Road #70/ Branch Pond Road. Forest Service Road #71 comes in on the right, and in a couple hundred feet, on the opposite side of the road is the Stratton Pond Trail parking lot.

It is nearly four miles to the pond. The map coordinates in the heading locates the shelter at Stratton Pond, near where the Long Trail meets the pond. It is another three quarters of a mile to the tenting area. Whether you stay in the tenting area or shelter, a Green Mountain Club caretaker will collect an overnight fee.

There is an old trail that connects to Bourn Pond, crossing the headwaters of the Winhall River, a true wilderness stretch of water that is as much a paternoster chain of beaver ponds as it is a brook. There are native brookies here, and the casting can be open in places. Because of the very heavy blowdown, and the lack of maintenance in this wilderness area, it is quite a challenging route and not recommended for any but the most hardened and terrain-savvy visitors.

Foul weather blows in at Stratton Pond

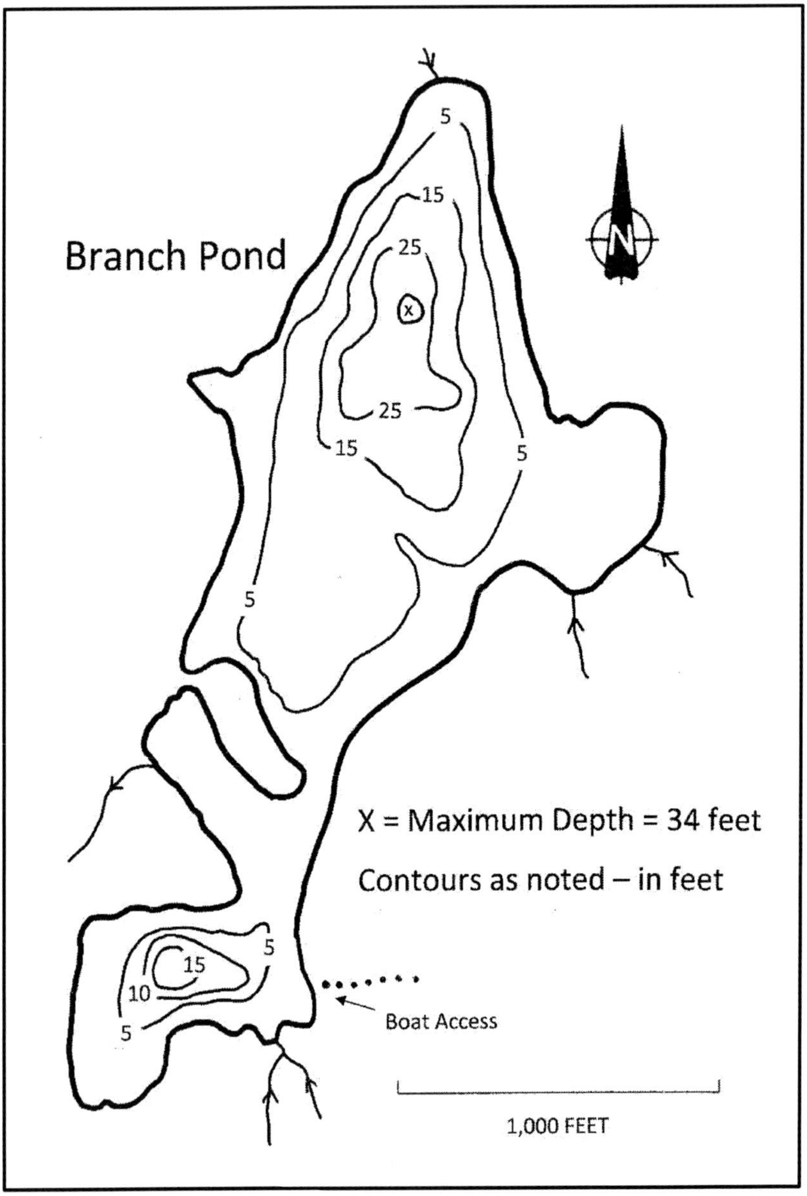
Branch Pond
5
15
25
x
25
15
5
5
N
X = Maximum Depth = 34 feet
Contours as noted – in feet
5
15
10
5
Boat Access
1,000 FEET

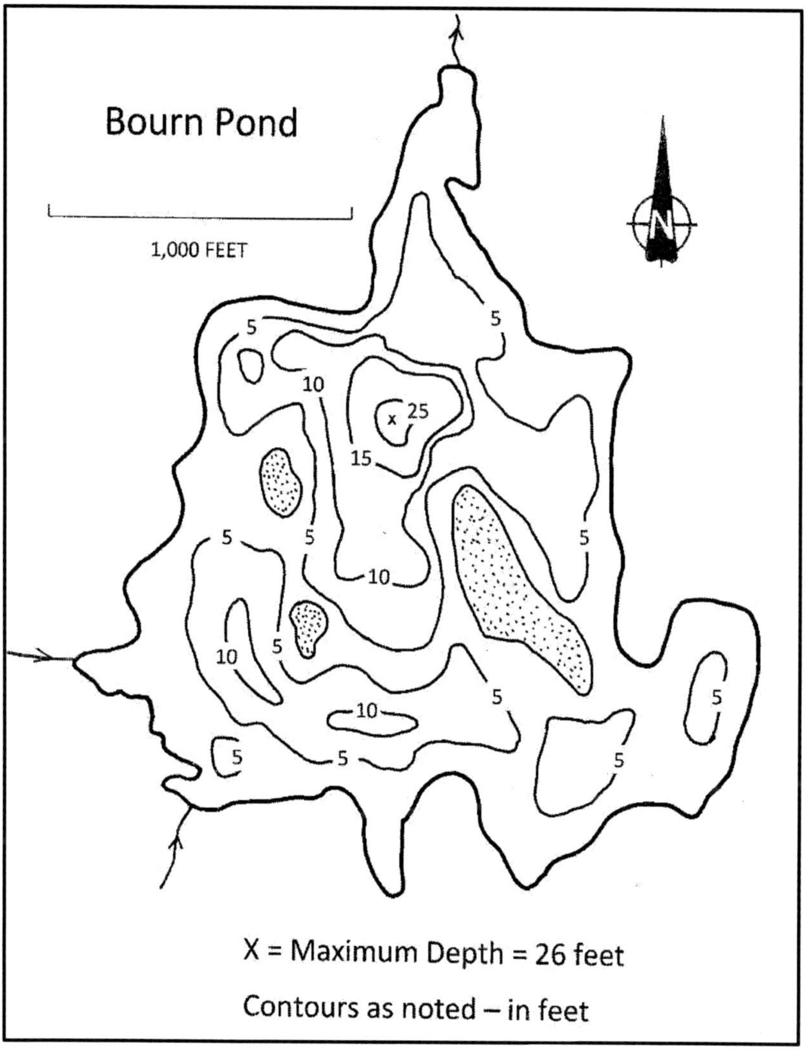
Bourn Pond
1,000 FEET
N
5
5
10
25
x
15
5
5
5
10
5
10
5
10
5
5
5
5
5
X = Maximum Depth = 26 feet
Contours as noted – in feet

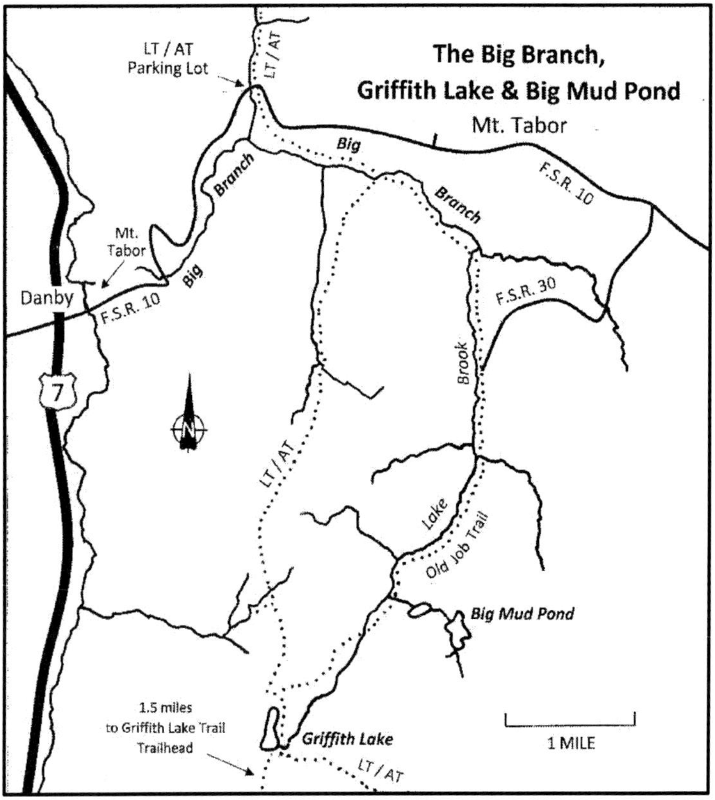
The Big Branch,
Griffith Lake & Big Mud Pond
Mt. Tabor
LT / AT
Parking Lot
LT / AT
Big
Branch
F.S.R. 10
Mt.
Tabor
Danby
F.S.R. 10
Big
Branch
F.S.R. 30
Brook
7
LT / AT
Lake
Old Job Trail
Big Mud Pond
1.5 miles
to Griffith Lake Trail
Trailhead
Griffith Lake
LT / AT
1 MILE

Big Branch, Big Mud Pond, and Griffith Lake

The Big Branch Wilderness, the Peru Peak Wilderness, and the White Rocks National Recreation Area encompass a little patch of southern Vermont that offers plenty of opportunity to chase backwoods brookies, as well as some wild browns and rainbows in an extraordinary angling environment. Although virtually all of this guidebook is focused on ponds, the moving water of the Big Branch cannot be ignored as a true trout hike. It offers a singular fishing experience.

All of these waters are most easily reached from Forest Service Road #10, a seasonally maintained road that is closed during the winter months, and runs between Mt. Tabor and North Landgrove. This road is not plowed, and winter can come early and stay late, so inquire with U.S.F.S. and check weather if you are planning on fishing the very extreme ends of the trout season.

Access to this area from the east makes for a longer haul to the fishing action than coming in from the west. If you are on the east side of the Green Mountains, start in Landgrove and take the Landgrove Road north. From the intersection of the Landgrove Road and Hapgood Pond Road, it is a little more than a half mile to where Little Michigan Road comes in on the left. Make the left and follow Little Michigan road for .7 miles and make the right turn onto Forest Service Road #10 (a.k.a Danby Mount Tabor Road.) From here it is just shy of seven miles to Forest Service Road #30, and another three and a half miles to the Long Trail Parking lot.

Coming to this area from the west is a shorter drive. Driving north or south on U.S. Route 7, you are looking for Mt. Tabor and the Brooklyn Road, which heads east into the village of Mt. Tabor. An excellent landmark is the Mt. Tabor Country Store which is located on the west side of U.S. Route 7, about seven hundred feet north of the Brooklyn Road. The store offers gas, a small selection of groceries, some basic fishing tackle and a deli with attending grill. The latter has always received my five diamond rating, but I'll confess the prelude has always included several days of eating trail food.

From Route 7, head east on Brooklyn Road (Forest Service Road #10) through the village of Mt. Tabor, crossing the Big Branch in about a mile. Another two miles of mountain road, and a memorable hairpin curve, and you will reach the Long Trail/Appalachian Trail parking lot. From here it is another three and a half miles to where Forest Service Road #30 comes in on the right.

Both of these are navigation points to the trout hikes that follow in this section.

Big Branch, N 43.3724 W 72.9626

Mt. Tabor (Long Trail Trailhead)

"Big Branch." The name itself implies something special and great. It doesn't disappoint. And, since it is right in the middle of the area in which these ponds are located, and runs through designated wilderness, it would be unthinkable to not address it.

More than two miles of this river flows through the wilderness that takes its name from this mountain stream. Nearly all of this guidebook is focused on lakes and ponds. By the time our streams reach any kind of significant size, roads and development are in attendance. The Big Branch Wilderness, and the two miles of river within it, provide a unique fishing destination. It is not a place for those weak of leg. Leave the fishing boots behind. It's hiking boots for the trail and off-trail, and sneakers or, even better, rock climbing high-cuts, for fishing and wet wading – where you *can* wade. Fish with a partner.

This is your typical tumbledown mountain stream but at a 10X macro-scale. Plunge pools have depths way out of proportions to their meager surface areas. They host brookies throughout, but in the lower sections there are browns, and the darkest rainbows on the planet – well, in Vermont anyway. These fish charge up from unseen

The Big Branch in August's low water conditions

depths to rip at a fly. They have only milliseconds to decide. It's a circumstance that always works in the angler's favor.

In many places an angler only has a few feet of "playground" before a hooked fish will take a ride down the next waterfall, leaving the angler to decide between a precarious chase downstream, or horsing it up -- either airborne or through the crush of the falls.

Here's a suggestion for a great day-trip on the Big Branch. Follow the directions above to the Long Trail/Appalachian Trail Parking Lot. There is an undeveloped and unmarked social trail that starts at the back of the parking lot, and follows the right bank of the Big Black Branch down to an ancient cement bridge abutment and the juncture with The Big Branch. This reach of stream is in the heart of the Big Branch Wilderness. The wilderness boundary lies about three quarters of a mile downstream, and about a mile and a half upstream, from this point. Downstream from here the angler will find those special rainbows in the mix with the brookies. Upstream it goes exclusively to brook trout. There has been no stocking in this reach of the stream in many years. The trout here are wild.

One can make a day of it, fishing downstream and out of the wilderness area, until the Forest Service bridge is in view, then fish back to the Big Black Branch, and a hike out. For an overnight stay, one could take the Long Trail south from this same parking lot to the Big Branch Shelter, a little over a mile hike. This shelter is maintained by the Green Mountain Club, and they describe it as a framed lean-to with floor space for eight. This might be a good place to settle for a few nights, and explore the options.

Griffith Lake, N 43.3033 W 72.9592

Griffith Lake lies astride the towns of Mt. Tabor and Peru. It is 13 acres in extent, and has an elevation of 2,634 feet. In most years 2,000 spring fingerling brookies have been planted in Griffith Lake, which like other high elevation lakes are short on suitable spawning areas, but have good growth with the stocked fish.

Griffith is among the highest of Vermont's trout ponds. Technically, Griffith Lake is within the White Rocks National Recreation Area, but is closely bounded by the Peru Peak and Big Branch Wilderness areas, in some cases as close as a hundred feet. The lake lies alongside the Long Trail/Appalachian Trail, so there is usually plenty of hiking traffic. However, in what seems a common characteristic of other popular lakes that adjoin the Long Trail, it is only a very small minority of these visitors who choose to fish. The Green Mountain Club maintains a tenting area on the east side of the lake. A nominal fee helps the GMC maintain the trail system –

including "keeping order" on these busiest of hiking routes.

The shortest route into Griffith Lake is to come from the south, but it is less interesting for an angler than coming from the north. To reach Griffith Lake from the north, follow the general directions to Forest Service Road #30, and take that road two and a quarter miles to its end at Lake Brook.

From here, the Old Job Trail follows Lake Brook upstream, heading three and a quarter miles south to Griffith Lake. It is a gradual trail, gaining a little more than seven hundred feet in elevation. Starting out as an obvious road, after some miles it gets more trail-like. I'll have to say, I've not ever met anyone else along this trail. The trail follows Lake Brook, whose plunge-pools hold some of the darkest-colored brookies I've ever seen. Their near sable backs contrast to the shocking vermilion of their lower flanks. It is easy to get distracted, and extend the hike way beyond reason, in trying to sample this little stream as you follow the trail.

At about the two-mile point the outlet from Little and Big Mud Ponds crosses the trail. (We'll be back here again, as we mark this as the jumping off point for the haul up to Big Mud Pond.)

For those of us who fish with flies, Griffith Lake is challenging to fish from shore. On the lake's west side a couple of small openings, and the log debris at its north, offer patches of open air in which to backcast. Waders, chest waders in particular, opens up the extent of reachable water. The ideal, of course, is to haul along a float tube.

Big Mud Pond, N 43.3153 W 72.9318

Big Mud Pond is a shallow, 15-acre pond, at an elevation of 2,620. Its maximum depth is five-plus feet. It lies in a trailless area of the town of Mt. Tabor. I have had this little gem all to myself every time that I have visited. This has included the 4th of July and Columbus Day, when a mere mile and a half away from where I lay my head, a score of Long Trail and Appalachian Trail hikers vied for a camping spot at Griffith Lake.

The size of the fish here is very much dependent on the time of year. They are snaky in the early spring, and colorful little footballs in the fall. 2,000 spring fingerlings are stocked annually.

Located in the Peru Peak Wilderness it is one of the most remote, and least visited trout ponds in the state. To get to Big Mud Pond, follow the directions to Griffith Lake (see above,) but stopping at this pond's outlet, about two miles from where you parked the car, at the Old Job Trail trailhead.

View from the campsite at Big Mud Pond

Technically the route goes through trailless wilderness, but there is a remnant trail that parallels the outlet, and an intermittent game trail leads to the pond. The latter is easier to follow on the way out as in, so I'll make no attempt at directing you to it. But, there is no getting lost, as you can stay pretty much within eyeshot of the water as you travel.

From the Old Job Trail, instead of immediately following the outlet upstream, backtrack north about fifty feet or so. Some heavy equipment has blocked off the start of an old trail with a small earthen berm. Go beyond the berm and find the old trail. It's a short but relatively steep climb to Little Mud Pond, about a thousand feet upstream. From Little Mud Pond you can just work your way north, and then east, keeping your eye on the shoreline of Little Mud Pond, and then, follow the outlet from Big Mud Pond. Right at the outlet of Big Mud Pond (near its right bank) a social campsite has been established. The exact latitude and longitude of the campsite are cited in the heading above.

For those of us who throw a fly around, there's a decent casting from shore at camp, especially if you can wade a little. There are several other casting perches to be had, though it's rough walking around the pond.

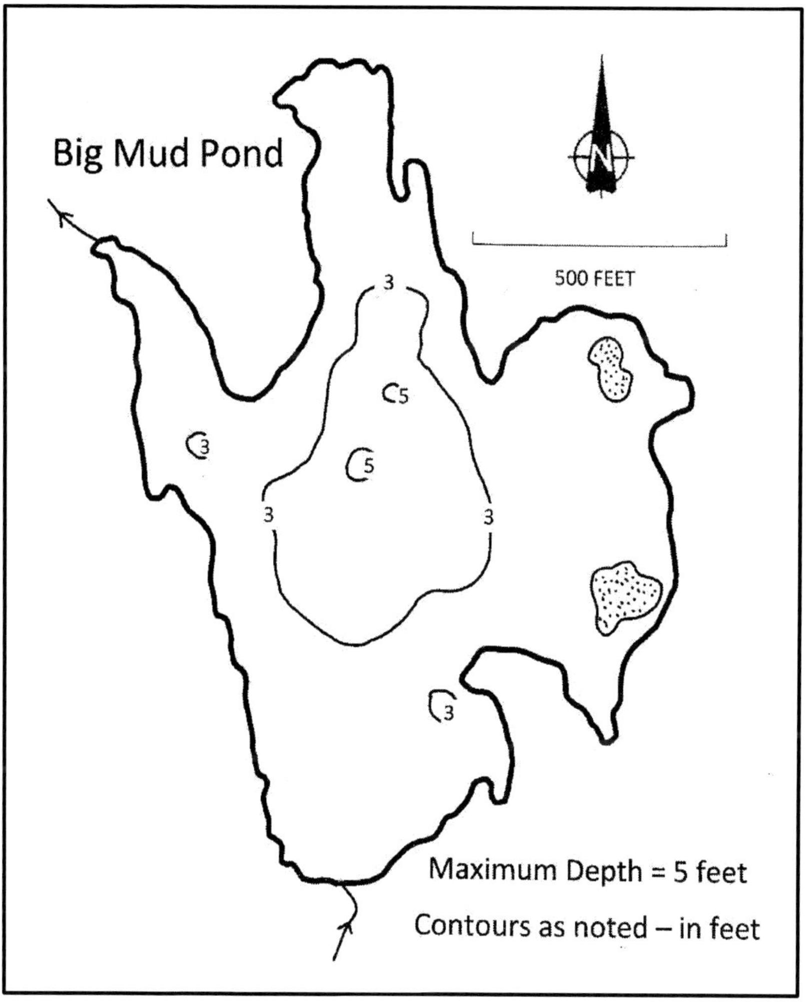
Big Mud Pond
N
500 FEET
3
5
5
3
3
3
3
Maximum Depth = 5 feet
Contours as noted – in feet

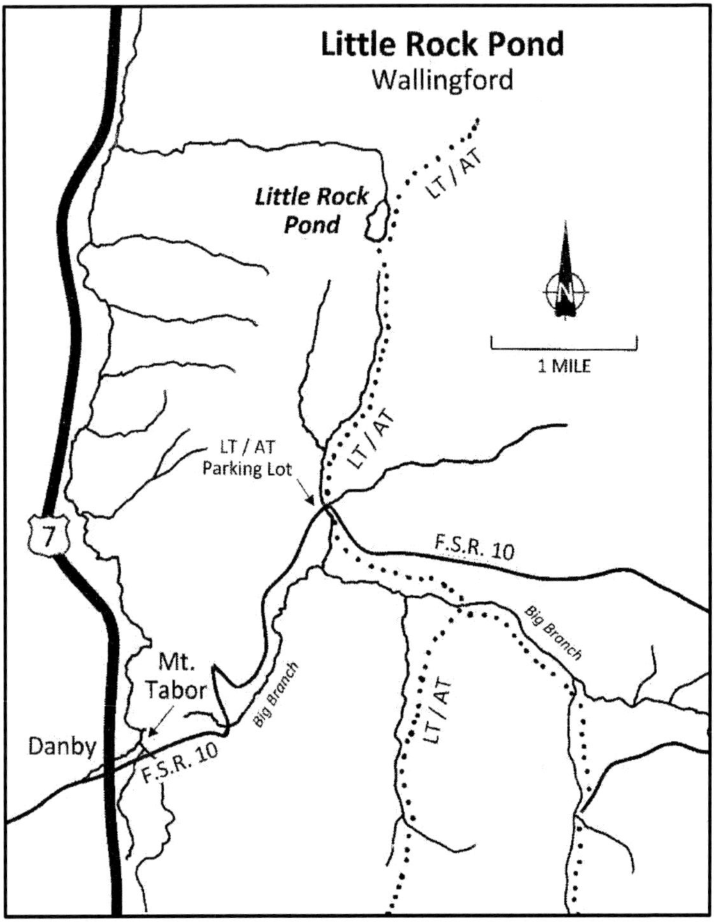
Little Rock Pond
Wallingford
LT / AT
Little Rock Pond
1 MILE
LT / AT
LT / AT
Parking Lot
7
F.S.R. 10
Big Branch
Mt.
Tabor
Big Branch
LT / AT
Danby
F.S.R. 10

Little Rock Pond, N 43.3981 W 72.9558

Little Rock Pond is in the town of Wallingford. It is 18 acres in size, a depth of 37 feet, and is at an elevation of 1,887 feet. An annual stocking of 2,000 spring fingerling brook trout has been the rule. This is one of several Vermont lakes in which these plantings of small trout produce nice catchable-sized fish – some a foot long or better. My theory is that, in this lake, they get fat on the enormous population of crayfish that thrive here.

Little Rock Pond is most easily accessed from the south. From the Long Trail Parking lot, which is referenced in the general directions in this section's introduction, take the trail north 2.25 miles, gradually climbing about 350 feet to the pond. The GPS coordinates in the heading above note where the trail hits the pond. If you are camping, an early arrival will ensure a spot at the shelter or tenting area (nearer the fishing) that are maintained by the Green Mountain Club. A nominal fee for overnight camping is required.

Little Rock Pond lies within the White Rocks National Recreation Area. It is located right along the Long Trail/Appalachian Trail, and is one of the busiest places for through-hikers, some on a journey on the Long Trail, others trekking the Appalachian Trail. Because of its ease of access and short hike, it's also popular with locals, and will even see a little fishing pressure in the spring. As summer unfolds much of the traffic consists of thru-hikers, and anglers are few.

There is good casting, some of it vertical, from the rock outcrops that occupy a nice piece of real estate on the southwestern shore. It is also a great perch from which to stalk trout using a good pair of polarized sunglasses. And, for fly anglers who pursue the "hex hatch" this is a truly great destination, as this mayfly hatch starts here in late June and early July, and continues for weeks. You can wade out in the muddy bottom of the southeast corner area to cast – and this location is perfect for those giant mayflies, because of its muddy bottom.

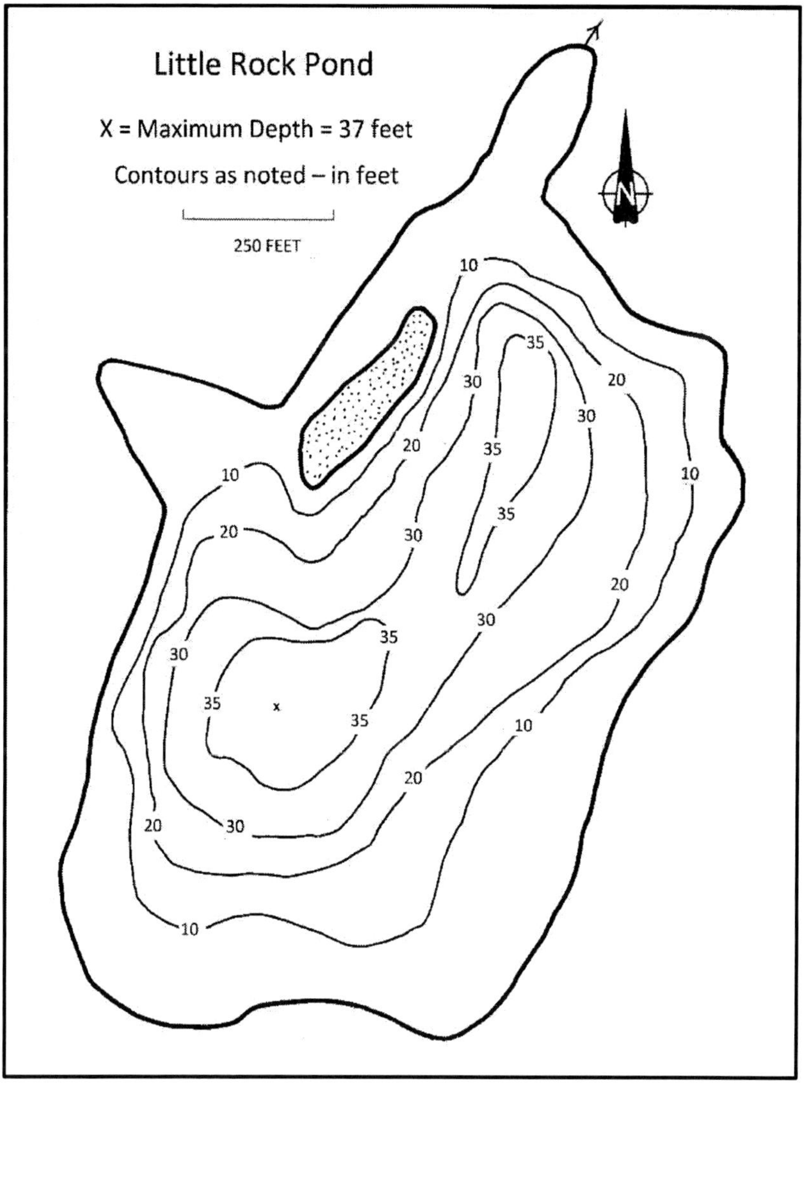
Little Rock Pond
X = Maximum Depth = 37 feet
Contours as noted – in feet
250 FEET
N
10
35
30
20
30
20
35
10
10
35
20
30
20
30
35
35
35
30
10
20
20
30
10

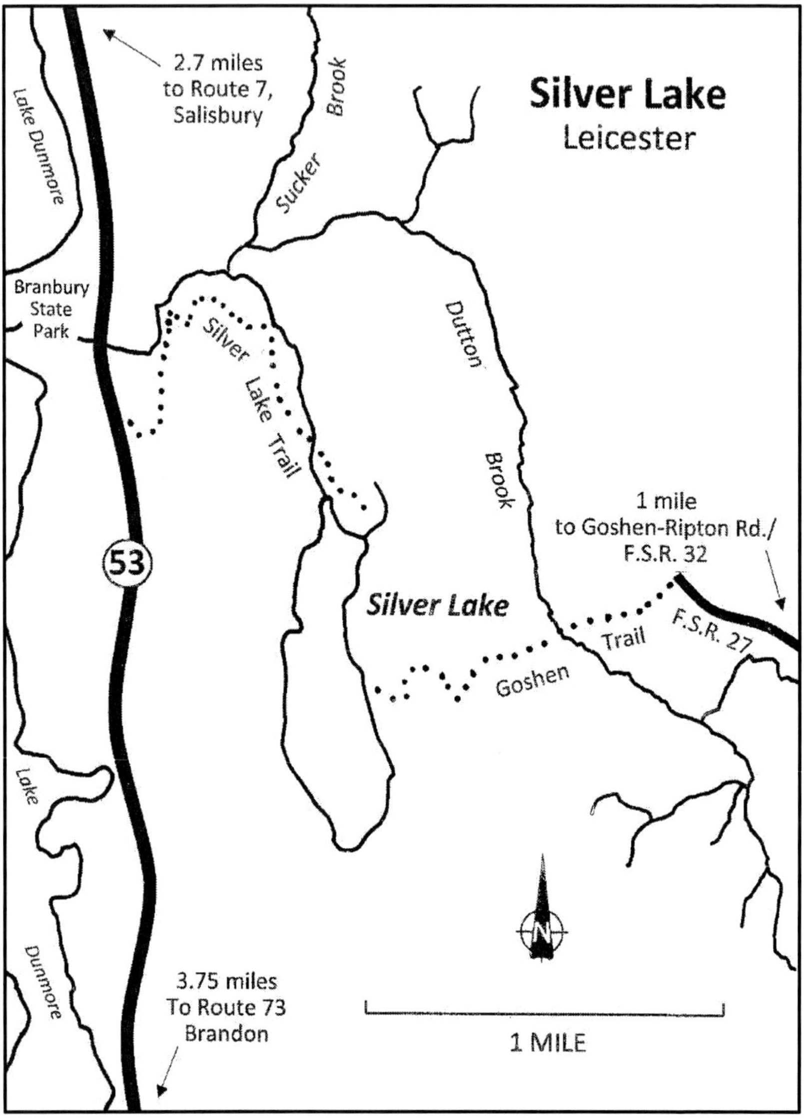
Silver Lake
Leicester
2.7 miles
to Route 7,
Salisbury
Sucker
Brook
Lake Dunmore
Branbury
State
Park
Silver
Lake
Trail
Dutton
Brook
1 mile
to Goshen-Ripton Rd./
F.S.R. 32
53
Silver Lake
Goshen
Trail
F.S.R. 27
Lake
Dunmore
N
3.75 miles
To Route 73
Brandon
1 MILE

Silver Lake, N 43.8970 W 73.0511

Silver Lake is in the town of Leicester. At 101 acres it is the second largest of the waterbodies addressed in this guidebook. It has an elevation of 1,248 feet, and a maximum depth of 69 feet. It has been regularly stocked. In the last few years the numbers of brook trout stocked have been bumped up to 1,200 – 1,600. These are nice brookies, 9-plus inches on average. These fish are joined by what has been a metronomic stocking of 500 rainbows each year. These are in the 10-plus inch range. There are also brown trout present from stockings in the previous decade.

This is a great destination for a first-time camper or a family. It is a beautiful location, a short hike, and there are 15 designated campsites, with picnic tables and fire pits. Perhaps most importantly, for those who may not yet be inclined to "dig a hole" for their latrine protocol, there are state-of-the-art pit toilets. It is also a great destination for a day-hike, if you are staying at nearby Branbury State Park, with their full-service campground.

The lake is located within the Green Mountain National Forest, and has two access points. One is to the west of the lake, with a trailhead located a half-mile south of the Branbury State Park's entrance. It is on the east side of State Route 53. From this trailhead it is about a six-hundred-foot climb to the lake. Five hundred feet of the climb is accomplished in the first half of the mile-and-a-half trail. (It's a road really.) The GPS coordinates designate "the beach," near the head of the dam. There are deep gorges and scenic overlooks adjacent to some portions of the trail, so youngsters need close supervision.

You can also hike to Silver Lake from Goshen. There is a well maintained dirt and gravel road that runs the eight miles or so between Ripton and Goshen: Forest Service Road #32/Goshen-Ripton Road. Coming from either Ripton or Goshen, the Silver Lake Road (Forest Service Road #27) joins from the west and heads west two miles to a gate and the trailhead parking lot. From here the Goshen Trail runs a little more than a half mile, and drops about 250 feet to the lake.

Here's an inspiration that needs a conspirator and a car drop. Some over-zealous, perhaps a little crazy, anglers will actually carry a jon-boat, a canoe, or kayak in from the Goshen side (all downhill) and then, when they finish fishing or camping, continue the downhill trek to the Route 53 trailhead, where they have parked transportation. This is not an easy feat, so know your limits. The short trail from Goshen is a *trail* trail, not the "road" that comes in from the Lake Dunmore side.

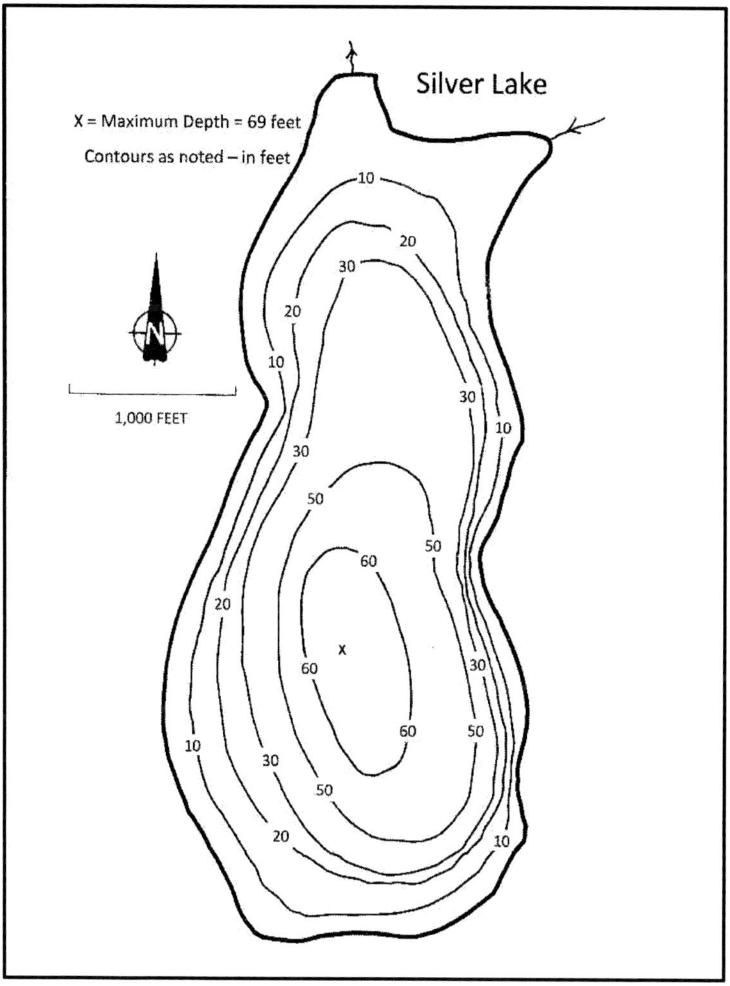
Silver Lake
X = Maximum Depth = 69 feet
Contours as noted – in feet
N
1,000 FEET
10
20
30
10
20
30
10
30
50
50
60
20
x
60
30
10
60
50
30
50
20
10

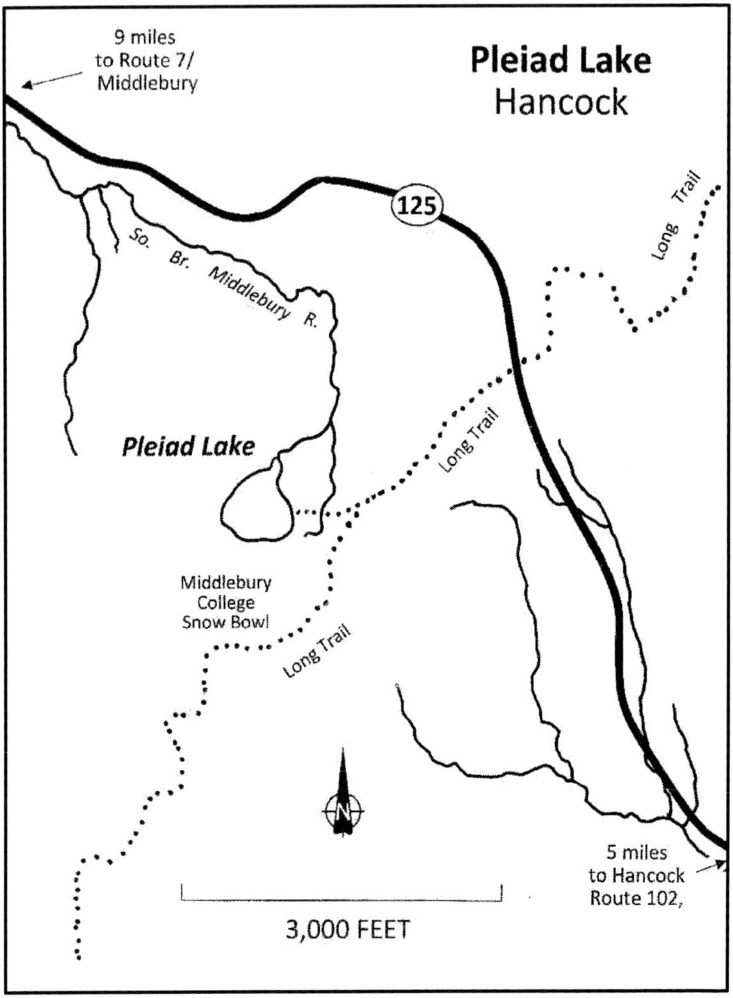
9 miles
to Route 7/
Middlebury
Pleiad Lake
Hancock
125
So. Br. Middlebury R.
Long Trail
Long Trail
Pleiad Lake
Middlebury
College
Snow Bowl
Long Trail
N
5 miles
to Hancock
Route 102,
3,000 FEET

Pleiad Lake, N 43.9341 W 72.9574

This 6-acre pond is located in the town of Hancock, just west of the Long Trail, about a half-mile southwest of where the Long Trail crosses State Route 125. It has an elevation of 2,160 feet. Fish & Wildlife has not stocked here for at least a dozen years. Wild brook trout were sampled in 2015.

The trailhead is located about 5.5 miles east of Ripton. There is a large pull-off parking lot and plenty of signage. Take the Long Trail south for about a half mile, where the Long Trail forks sharply to the left, and straight on is the spur trail to Pleiad Lake. Take the spur trail, which shortly crosses a streamlet, proceeding 0.1 mile to the pond. The GPS coordinates mark the prominent rock outcrop at the pond's east side.

Although this is a short hike, there is definitely some up and down, including a very steep section that rapidly drops a hundred feet of elevation in a short distance. This will present a challenge to those with "elder balance" or old knees, who are unaccustomed to walking trails.

There is good casting from the large rock outcrop on the pond's east side, as well as along the narrow bedrock edge of the pond, south of the big rock outcrop.

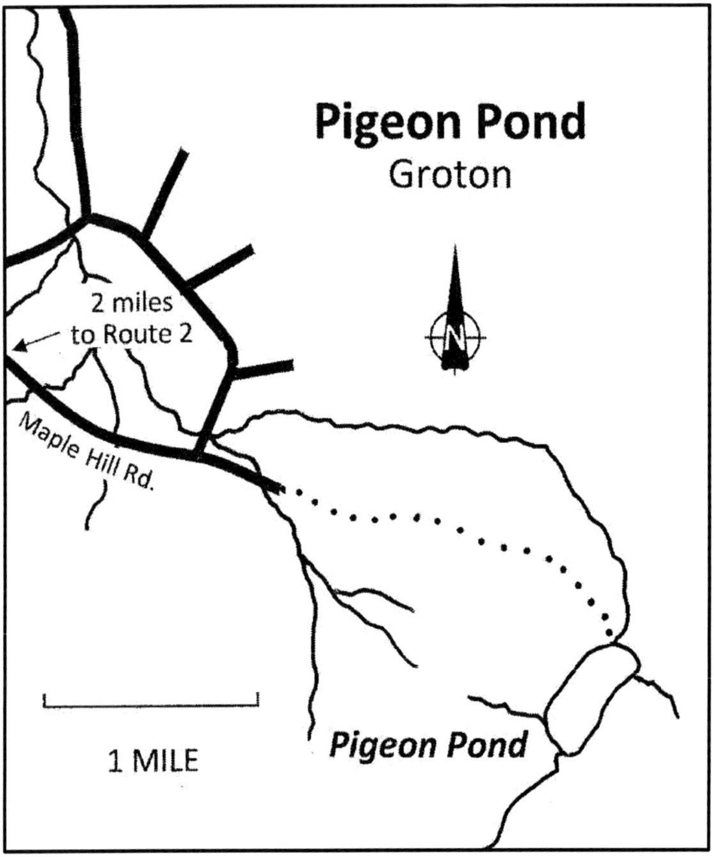
Pigeon Pond
Groton
2 miles
to Route 2
N
Maple Hill Rd.
1 MILE
Pigeon Pond

Pigeon Pond, N 44.2510 W 72.3258

Pigeon Pond is in Groton. It has 689 acres and a maximum depth of 21 feet. Its elevation is 1,958 feet. This pond has received regular annual plantings of 500 fingerling brookies. These do very well. The 2008 sampling found 100% of the trout to be wild, averaging 9.5 inches, with a maximum length of 13.1 inches.

Pigeon Pond's inclusion in this book was debatable, not for any shortcoming of trout, but rather because access is private and gated. Travel by foot, however, is permitted. If you don't own a camp on the pond, this makes it foot-access only, a criterion for inclusion in this guidebook, the other being the presence of trout. The easiest way to direct you is from U.S. Route 2. Take Main Street east in Plainfield, continuing on to a left fork and onto Maple Hill Road. Stay on Maple Hill Road for almost three miles. You will pass Holt Road on your left; stay to the right. In another mile and a half Holt Road loops back again on your left. At this juncture continue straight; the road name changes here to Pigeon Pond Road. In about a half mile you will reach the road's end. From here it's about a mile and three-quarters to the north end of the pond.

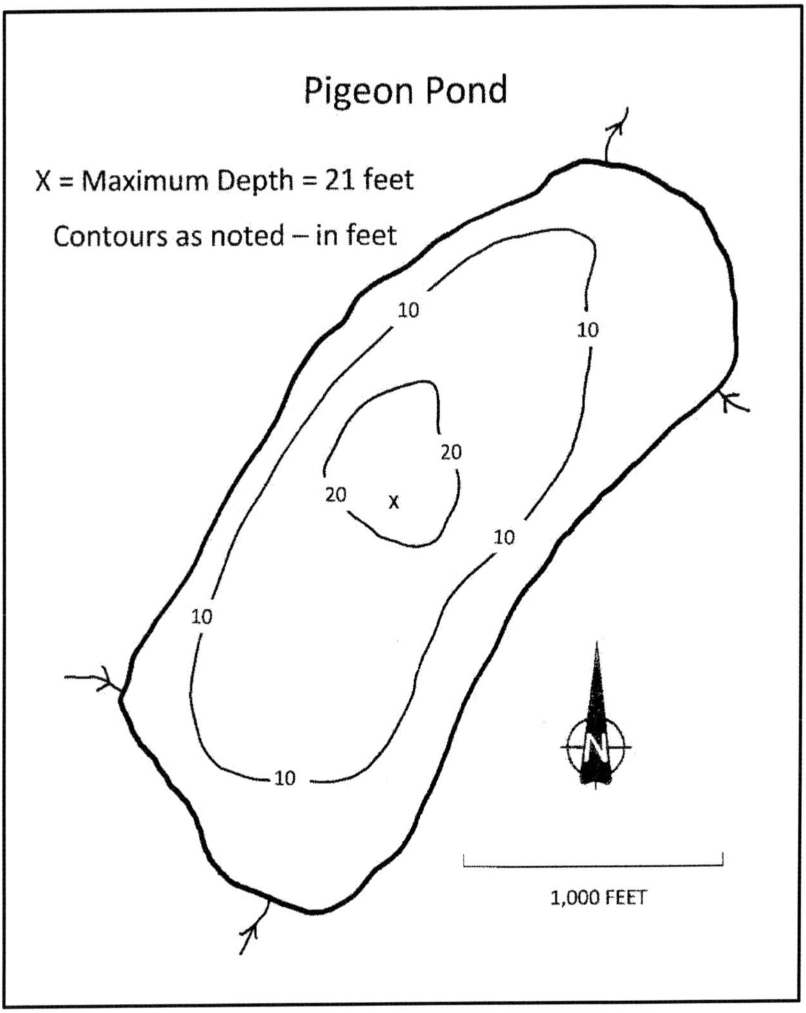
Pigeon Pond
X = Maximum Depth = 21 feet
Contours as noted – in feet
10
10
20
20
X
10
10
10
N
1,000 FEET

Notes

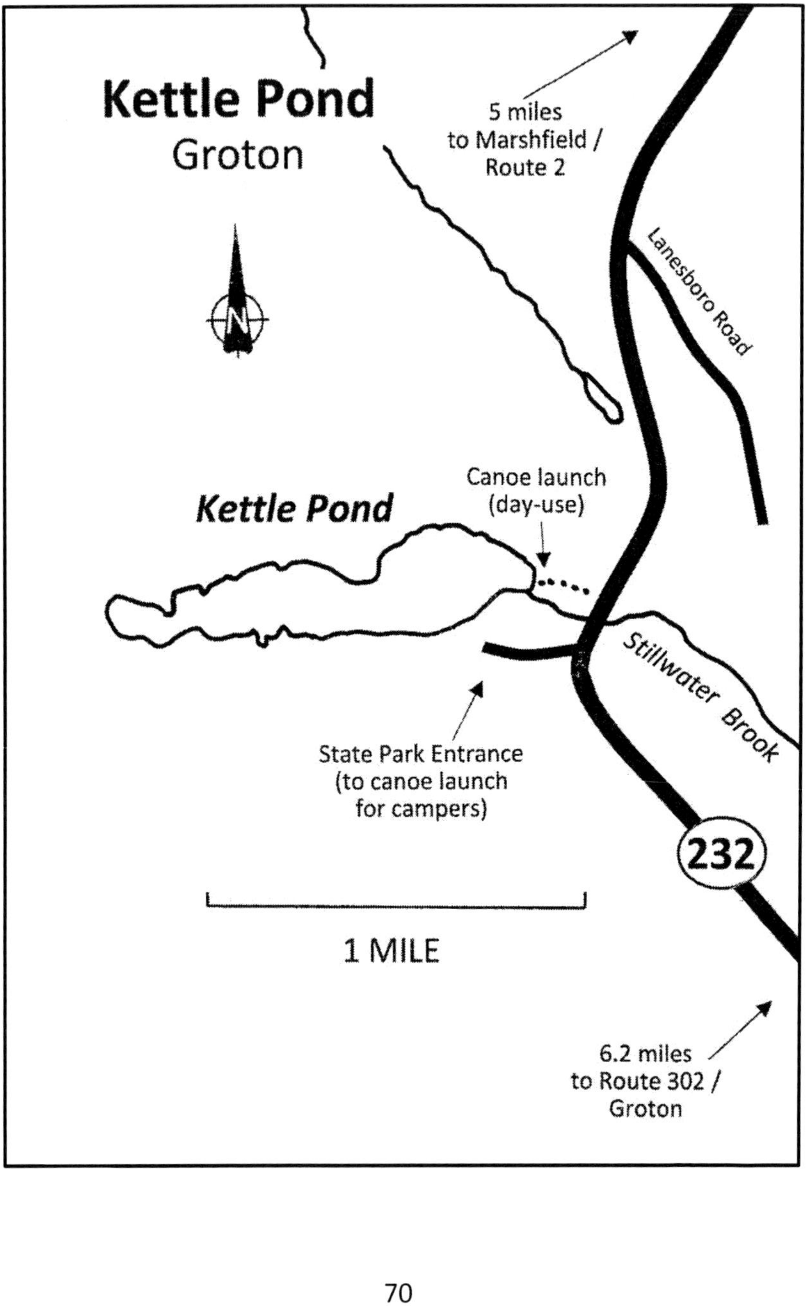
Kettle Pond
Groton
5 miles
to Marshfield /
Route 2
Lanesboro Road
Canoe launch
(day-use)
Kettle Pond
Stillwater Brook
State Park Entrance
(to canoe launch
for campers)
232
1 MILE
6.2 miles
to Route 302 /
Groton

Kettle Pond, N 44.2952 W 72.3049

Kettle Pond is in the town of Groton, and is the largest of the waterbodies included here: 109 acres. Its elevation is 1,445 feet, and it has a maximum depth of 18 feet. This pond sees an annual stocking of 1,000 rainbows generally in the 10-inch range, but in 2020 only 800 were put in. For those who may occasionally go slumming for smallmouth bass, this pond also holds some good ones.

The pond is the central feature of Kettle Pond State Park, which is located within the Groton State Forest. You should know there is a day-use fee for visitation, and the fee allows access to the several state parks in the Groton State Forest. You can register at New Discovery State Park. A portion of Kettle Pond State Park is dedicated to organized group camping, but of interest to the freelance angler are the day-use launch and the "remote campsites." Seven lean-to sites and one tent site are accessible by watercraft with a short portage.

If you are just day-tripping you can access the pond from a parking area, immediately off State Forest Road 232. If you are coming from the south (from Route 302,) the parking area is on the left, one and three quarter miles north of the Boulder Beach Road. Coming from the north (from Route 2/Marshfield) it is on the right, one mile south of Lanesboro Road. The boat access is a short walk, and the cited GPS coordinates designate the approximate location of the trailhead at the northwest end of the parking lot on Route 232. The portage is a little more than a tenth of a mile.

For overnight stays, you must also register. If you are registered for a campsite, you can launch your canoe or non-powered craft from the campground itself. It is a much shorter haul. The campground's entrance is just a couple hundred feet south of the Route 232 parking lot. (Please note again that registrations are at nearby New Discovery State Park.)

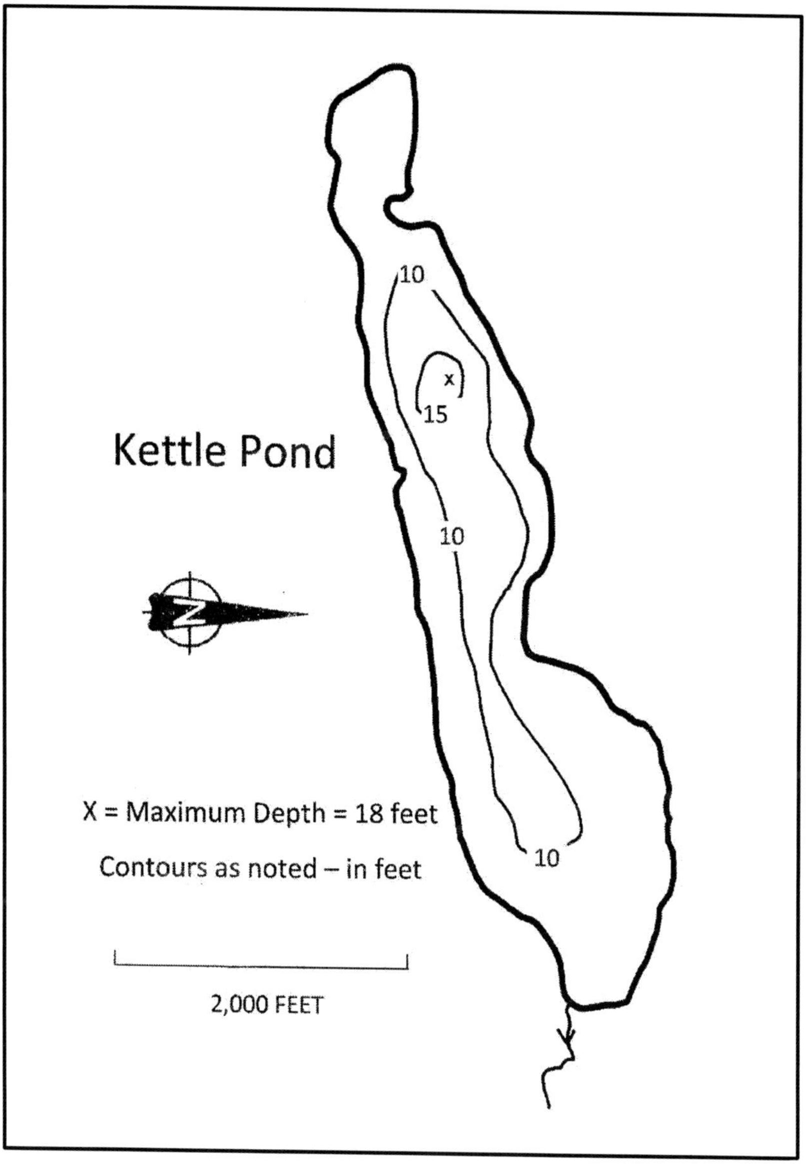
Kettle Pond
10
x
15
10
10
X = Maximum Depth = 18 feet
Contours as noted – in feet
2,000 FEET

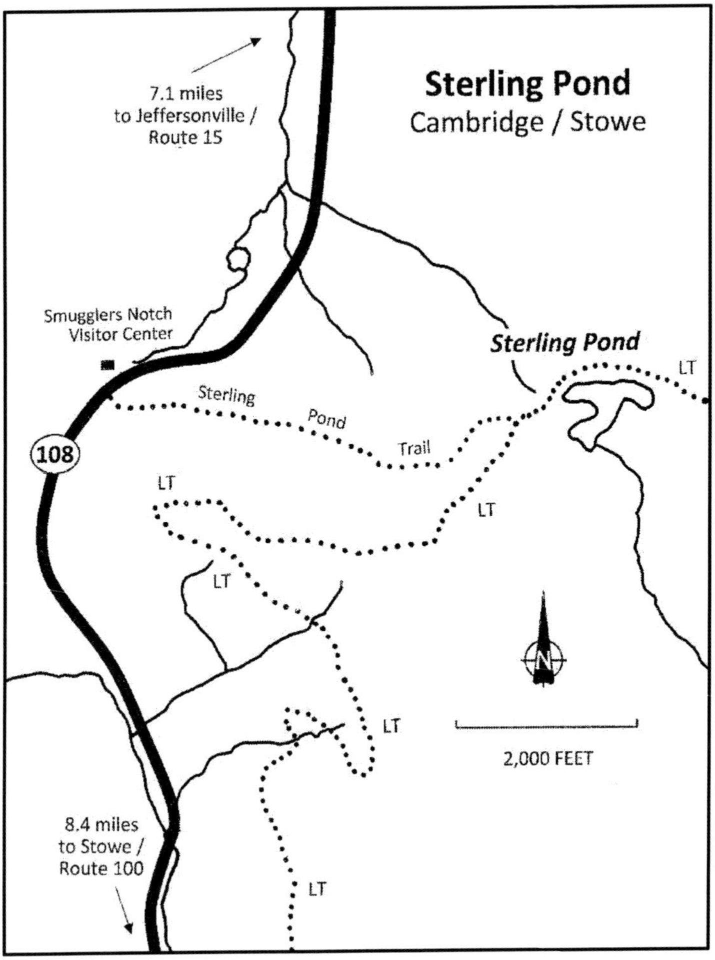

Sterling Pond
Cambridge / Stowe
7.1 miles
to Jeffersonville /
Route 15
Smugglers Notch
Visitor Center
Sterling Pond
LT
Sterling
Pond
Trail
108
LT
LT
LT
LT
2,000 FEET
8.4 miles
to Stowe /
Route 100
LT

Sterling Pond, N 44.5564 W 72.7763

Sterling Pond, Stowe/Cambridge covers eight acres, and is 26 feet deep at its maximum. Located at an elevation of 3,019 feet, it is the state's highest trout pond.

By employing Smuggler's Notch Resort's chairlifts, Sterling gets stocked with catchable-sized trout. Over the last decade, the annual numbers have ranged from 200 to 1,000. Their size has ranged from 8.5 to 9 inches. Most recent stockings (2018 -2020) have been at the 300-level, because some stunting has been reported with higher levels of stocking.

Sterling Pond lies along the Long Trail, and is most easily accessed by a one-mile steep climb from Smugglers Notch, following the Sterling Pond Trail. This leaves the east side of Route 108, a short distance south of the Smugglers Notch Visitor Center. This trail meets the Long Trail on the ridge, and the pond is a 0.1 mile hike north (left) on the Long Trail. The GPS coordinates designate the point where the Long Trail skirts the pond at an open area, which offers some of the best casting for the fly angler on foot. The caveat here is that you have to mind your backcast – there is a lot of hiking traffic behind you.

The Green Mountain Club maintains a busy shelter at the pond, and there is a nominal fee for an overnight stay.

An early arrival will ensure a place in the shelter. I do not recommend walking into or out of this pond after dark. Even with a good headlamp. It is about an 850-foot climb, and in places, you may be required to use your hands to balance. Think about overnight in the GMC shelter, or day tripping from nearby Smuggler's Notch Resort.

A float tube plies the water of Sterling Pond

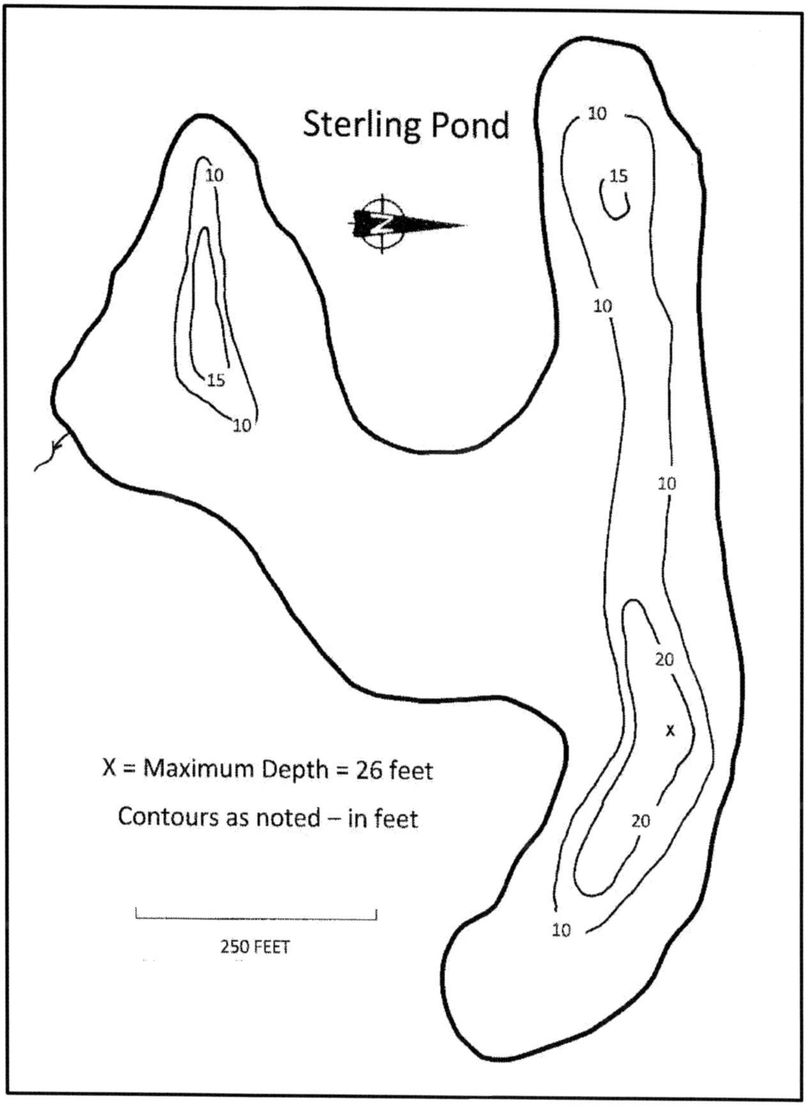
Sterling Pond
10
15
10
10
15
10
10
20
x
20
10
X = Maximum Depth = 26 feet
Contours as noted – in feet
250 FEET

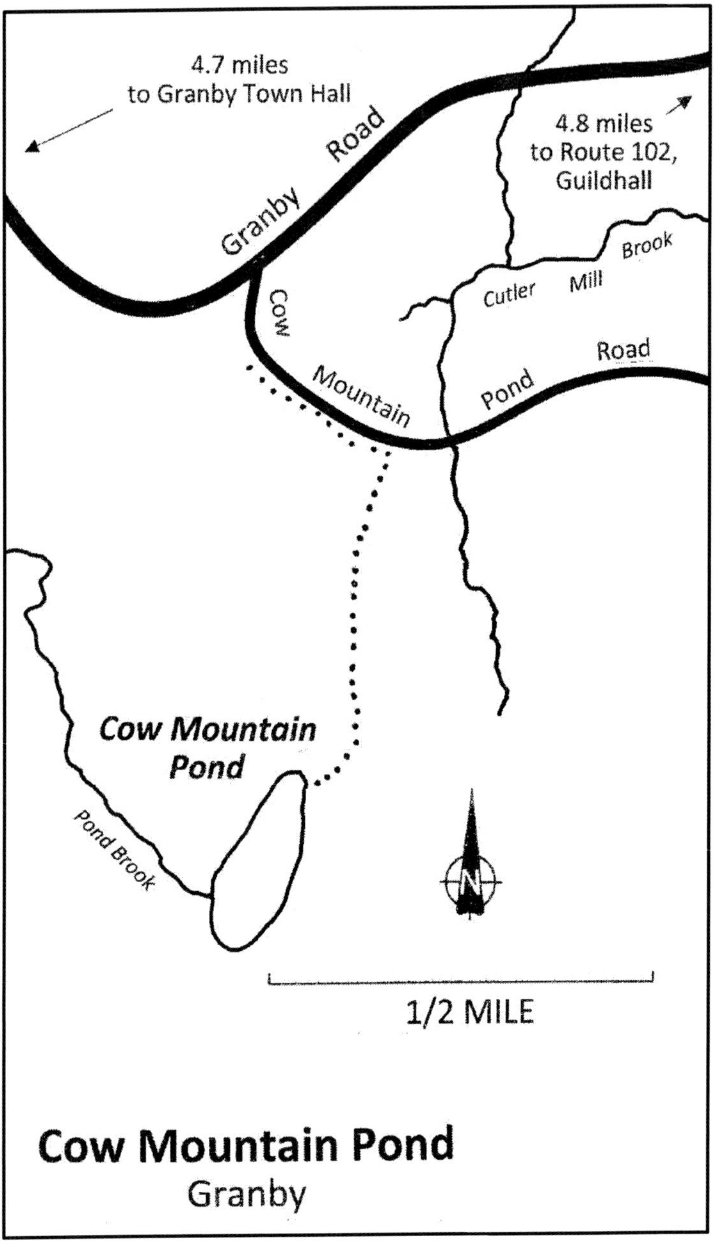
4.7 miles
to Granby Town Hall
Granby Road
4.8 miles
to Route 102,
Guildhall
Cutler Mill Brook
Cow Mountain Pond Road
Cow Mountain
Pond
Pond Brook
N
1/2 MILE
Cow Mountain Pond
Granby

Cow Mountain Pond, N 44.5633 W 71.7008

There is no stocking in this pond. In 2011, 100% of the sample trout were wild, and prettier fish are hard to find.

This is a 10-acre walk-in pond in the town of Granby. It has a maximum depth of 26 feet and an elevation of 2,057 feet. It is on a well-marked trail. The GPS coordinates above mark where the trail reaches the pond. (The GPS coordinates marking where Cow Mountain Pond Road joins the Granby Road are N 44.5725 W 71.7018.) Please do not park beyond the designated sign.

In a custom that has spanned decades, there has been a boat left for communal use, usually right where the trail meets the pond. On my last trip there, not only was the jon-boat watertight, some thoughtful benefactor had actually left a life preserver for communal use, as well. Courtesy requires returning the boat to where you found it.

There is a nice picnic area near the outlet on the southwest side of the pond. The opening in the forest here, as well as a little spit of land, affords a rare place to backcast, if you're just wearing hiking boots. Check with the town about fire permits and camping.

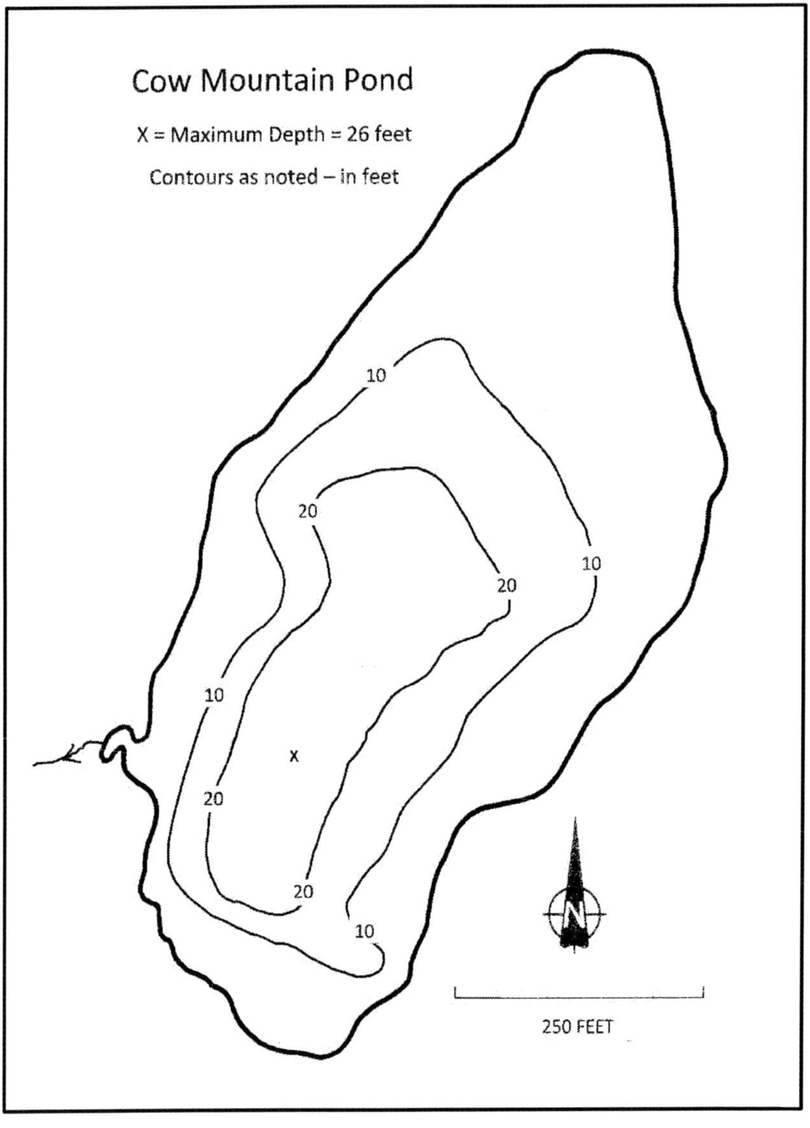
Cow Mountain Pond
X = Maximum Depth = 26 feet
Contours as noted – in feet
10
20
20
10
10
x
20
20
10
N
250 FEET

View of Cow Mountain Pond from "picnic clearing"

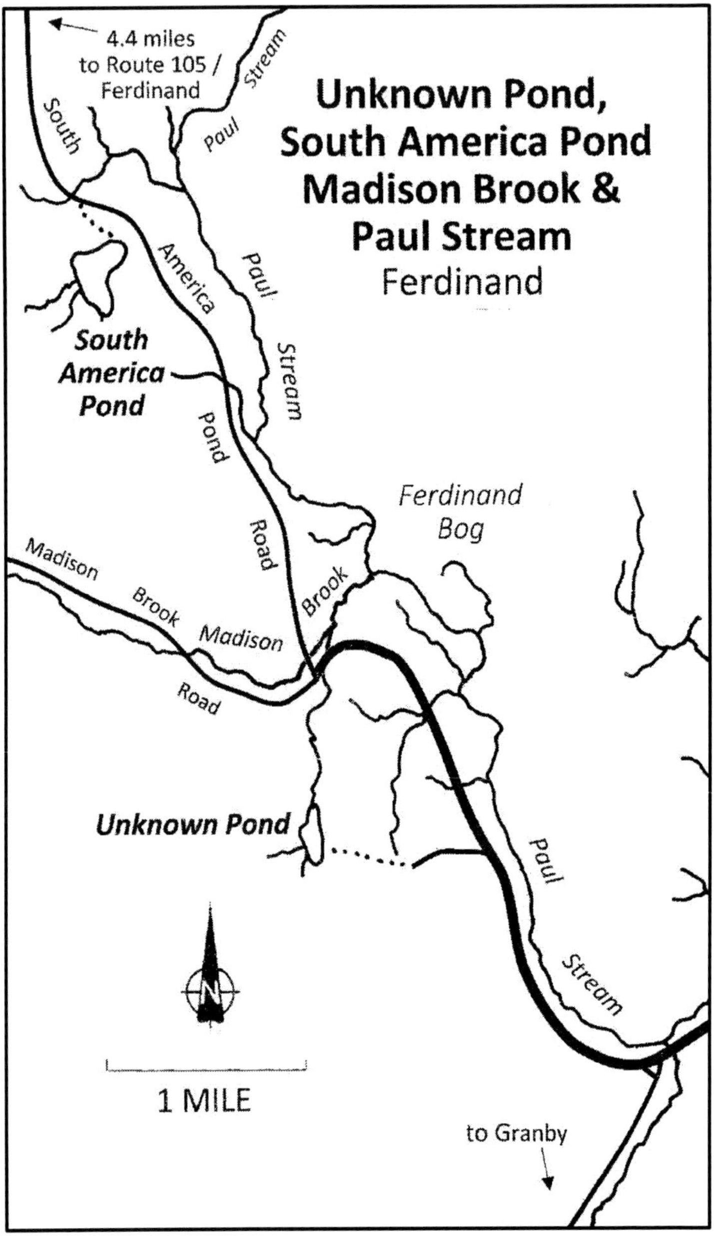
Unknown Pond,
South America Pond
Madison Brook &
Paul Stream
Ferdinand
4.4 miles
to Route 105 /
Ferdinand
South
America
Pond
Road
Paul
Stream
South
America
Pond
Ferdinand
Bog
Madison
Brook
Madison
Road
Unknown Pond
1 MILE
to Granby

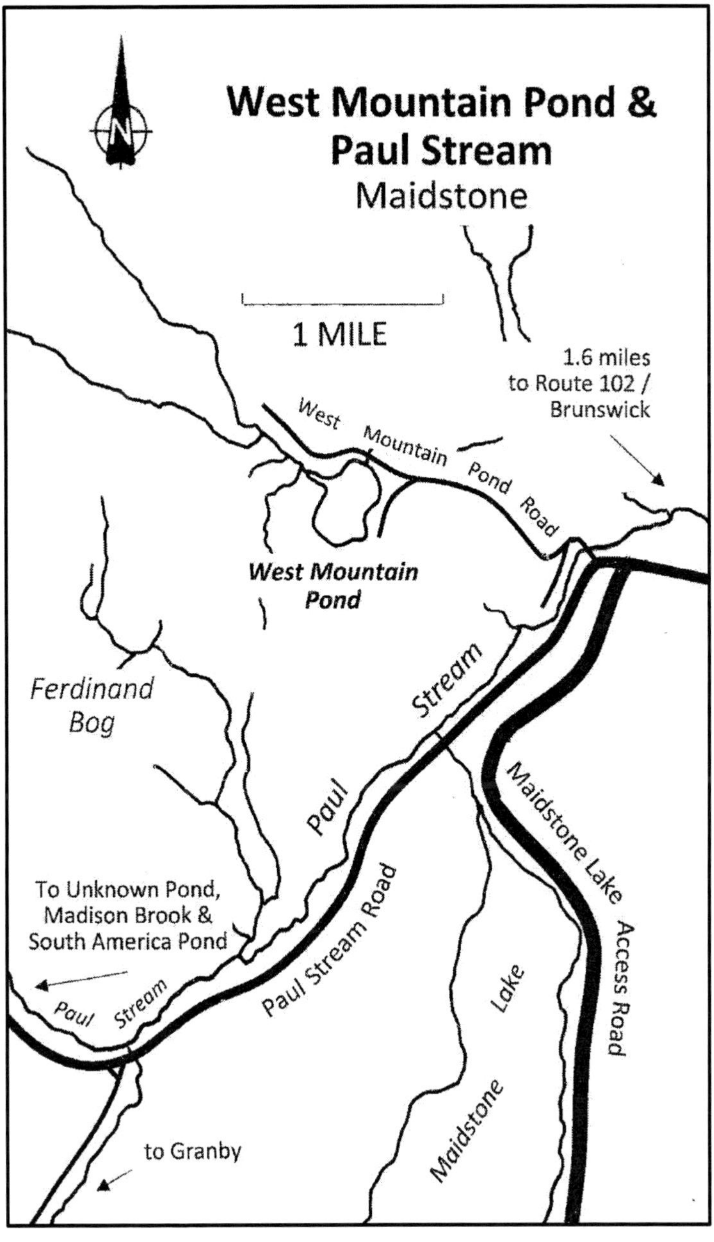
West Mountain Pond &
Paul Stream
Maidstone
N
1 MILE
1.6 miles
to Route 102 /
Brunswick
West Mountain Pond Road
West Mountain
Pond
Ferdinand
Bog
Paul Stream
Maidstone Lake Access Road
Paul Stream Road
To Unknown Pond,
Madison Brook &
South America Pond
Paul Stream
Maidstone Lake
to Granby

Lower reaches of Paul Stream get annual stockings

West Mountain Pond, Unknown Pond, Madison Brook, Paul Stream, and South America Pond (Ferdinand)

The area west and northwest of Maidstone Lake, in the town of Maidstone, hosts a few choice destinations for backwoods trout fishing. Much of it on the south side of Route 105 is encompassed within the West Mountain Wildlife Management Area.

The area around Maidstone Lake is the jumping off point for accessing these fishing holes. A large chunk of Maidstone Lake's shoreline is the site of Maidstone State Park, where you will find 25 lean-to's and 34 tent/RV sites. For those inclined for less adventurous camping, this is a great place to stage and camp for day-hikes into this region of Vermont. Another campsite, one that I refer to as the O-K Corral, lies near the northern end of South America Pond Road at N 44.7482 W 71.7507. There is dry level ground here and a nifty pit toilet. Be advised, however, there is also a healthy population of wood ticks, because the site was developed by and is used by horseback travelers. Absent horses, there are eight or nine hitching posts that you can use to rig a low tarp.

The road network that provides access to the area is not well marked with conventional road signs, and over time road conditions can vary. Except on the Maidstone Lake

Access Road, where 30 mph is a reasonable speed, driving above 20 mph is asking for trouble, especially in the spring. Through freeze-thaw action, large rocks poke their heads up on the road, like immovable icebergs, ready to puncture your gas tank. Other large rocks are completely missing in action. They seemed to have evaporated or been beamed-up, and only their gaping holes remain. Culverts collapse, or are washed away entirely, leaving trenches deep enough to face-plant your car.

Taking editor's privilege for the sake of clarity, and trying to avoid placing the reader at triple intersections, all of which say "South America Pond Road," let's come at these waters from the Connecticut River Valley. At any rate, it's a scenic and wondrous drive through some of Vermont's most undeveloped landscapes. West Mountain Pond would be the first trout hike we would encounter.

West Mountain Pond, N 44.6923 W 71.6632

West Mountain Pond is in the town of Maidstone. It has 60 acres at an elevation of 1,232 feet. Its maximum depth is 12 feet. There is no stocking in West Mountain Pond. Wild brook trout are present and are probably spawning in the tributaries. In 2017, Vermont Fish & Wildlife and Trout Unlimited added wood to one of the tributaries.

To access this pond, from the Connecticut River Valley in the town of Brunswick, leave State Route 102 and take the Maidstone Lake Access Road west. At about two and a quarter miles Paul Stream Road comes in on the right. Take the right turn, and follow Paul Stream Road for about 800 feet, where West Mountain Road comes in on the right. Make the right, shortly crossing a bridge over Paul Stream. In about a hundred feet, make a left, continuing to follow West Mountain Road. In 0.2 miles, take the right fork, staying with West Mountain Road. (Goodwin Camp Road is on the left fork.) In 1.2 miles more, take another right fork to stay on West Mountain Road. (Mayberry Road goes left.) Continue about 0.4 miles to parking, just beyond the pond's outlet, on the right, at approximately at N 44.6928 W 71.6612. The narrow, root-bumpy trail that leads to the pond is on the left side of the road, about 600 feet further, at approximate coordinates N 44.6923 W 71.6632. It's only about 125 feet to the pond. If you are launching craft or have lots of gear, you can drop it all at the trailhead, and return your vehicle to the parking area.

Unknown Pond, N 44.6650 W 71.7225

This Unknown Pond is in the town of Ferdinand. It covers 12 acres, having a maximum depth of 13 feet. Its elevation is 1,668 feet. This pond, with its secretive name, gets a customary stocking of about 500 fall fingerling brookies. An exception to the usual, the stocking was not accomplished in 2020. In 2010, 19% of the sample were wild, averaging 9.7 inches, so these fish are doing very well.

Unknown Pond from the east shore, near a camp

Directions to Unknown Pond are the same as above (to West Mountain Pond,) except that you stay on Paul Stream Road, and do not follow West Mountain Road over the bridge that crosses Paul Stream. Continue past West Mountain Pond Road on the right, and follow Paul Stream Road as it follows Paul Stream on its right. From the juncture of West Mountain Road, it is about two miles to where you will see a gravel pit on your left, and a road coming in on your right. (It is also Paul Stream

Road!) Ignore it, and continue straight on, along Paul Stream Road. In another one and three-quarter miles, you will cross Granby Stream. In less than a hundred feet, bear right at the fork and continue on Paul Stream Road, with the stream on your right. (This is another place where there are two roads, both called Paul Stream Road.)

From the bridge that crosses Granby Stream, continue northerly on Paul Stream Road, approximately 1.7 miles and turn left onto an unmarked camp road at N 44.6638 W 71.7057. Drive past the camp and park at the gravel pit at N 44.6619 W 71.7115. There is a trail that runs from the gravel pit up to a camp on the pond, about three-quarters of a mile walk, climbing up about 250 feet to a high point, about five hundred feet shy of the lake, and then down quickly a hundred feet or so, ending at a camp. There is a good place to cast on shore in front of the camp. If the camp is occupied, ask permission. If no one is home, practice "no trace casting."

By custom, a "social boat" has been stowed on the east side of the pond, well north of the camp. A rough trail edges the pond.

You can also come in to this pond from the west with less climbing. Returning to Paul Stream Road and the unmarked camp road, continue northerly another 1.7 miles, where South America Pond Road comes in on the right. Stay straight. You are now on Madison Brook Road, and in another half mile you will cross the powerline. Powerline Road comes in on the left. Make the left, and take the Powerline Road south. Find parking (where you can,) about three quarters of a mile from where you started down Powerline Road. Unknown Pond lies due east, just over a quarter of a mile and one hundred feet downhill. This is a ramble that will put you on the west side of the pond – the boggy side. You should have your navigation tools (and savvy) handy. There is a hard-to-follow trail, and an even harder-to-find trailhead, but you should just count on bushwhacking. Take a bearing on your map and have fun. It's a short haul.

Madison Brook and Paul Stream

In Vermont, after two and a half centuries of settlement, there is hardly any stream of significant size that isn't paralleled by a road. The two streams addressed here are no exception to that, but in one case you have to do some off-road walking to get to the best fishing, and in the other the road is gated for most of the year. In either case, if you are visiting this group of ponds, these streams are at your doorstep, and you are not likely to have a lot of company as you fish them.

In recent years Vermont Fish & Wildlife has strategically added large woody material to portions of these streams, and the habitat is looking much improved, as are the trout populations, which have increased both in number and size.

Madison Brook

Although this book has clearly focused on still water destinations, it would be a real oversight not to include a mention of two of the major streams in this watershed.

A sun-dappled stretch of Madison Brook

The lowermost reach of Madison Brook sees an annual stocking of some 400 catchable-size brook trout, from the

Madison Brook Bridge downstream to its mouth at Paul Stream. This provides a nice stretch of stocked stream, including its tightly meandering last reach, just before it enters Paul Stream. Upstream is water of a different character and home to wild brook trout.

Following directions, as above to Unknown Pond, you can make the right hand turn, north onto South America Pond Road from where it joins Madison Brook and Paul Stream Roads. You can immediately see the new, sturdy bridge that crosses Madison Brook about two hundred feet away. From this same intersection, you can continue straight on Madison Brook Road, passing the powerline and its road. If it is summer the road is gated, shortly after you pass the Powerline Road. Find parking and start walking up Madison Brook Road. The latter follows Madison Brook steeply, offering nearly a mile and a half of lonely fishing for wild brook trout.

Paul Stream

Paul Stream has its source on slopes of West Mountain and runs about fifteen miles to the Connecticut River. The unfortunate thing is that a good stretch of it runs through some boggy real estate. This increases the water temperatures too much to be very favorable to wild trout.

Brookies are stocked every year. These are nice 9-inch fish, and their numbers have ranged from 1,600 to 1,900 annually. In the past these were stocked both above and below Ferdinand Bog, but the fish above the bog have been doing so well that they have discontinued stocking in this reach.

There are various access points to reach Paul Stream's upper section. Driving north about a mile and a half on South America Pond Road, from the junction of Paul Stream Road and South America Pond Road, you will cross the outlet of South America Pond. Roughly speaking, at this point Paul Stream is located about a 750-foot bushwhack to the east. Ferdinand Bog's northern terminus is also located about here, so from this point upstream, you have about a mile's fishing until you hit the North Branch of Paul Stream, and another mile of fishing upstream, before you hit any crossing road. The North Branch itself offers a mile of reclusive fishing from its junction with the main stem, upstream until it crosses South America Pond Road.

Have your map and compass, so you don't get turned around. Find good parking places and explore. All along this stretch, you will find enough of a hike to the stream to leave the crowds behind. In the area where the North Branch joins Paul Stream, you will find some of the loneliest fishing in Vermont. This is not the easiest water in which to cast flies, but there are places that do open up, and even short-line casting or dapping can produce fish.

There is plenty of water you will not have to share, below Ferdinand Bog, as well. From the area roughly around the Unknown Pond camp road, downstream to the Connecticut, there are miles of little-fished water.

South America Pond, N 44.7070 W 71.7452

This 29-acre pond sits at an elevation of 1,751 feet. It is shallow for its size, with a maximum depth of only 6 feet. South America Pond is usually stocked with about 1,000 fall fingerling brookies. In the annual stockings, the fish are three to five inches in length. In 2010, 75% of the sample trout were wild, and averaged 7.8 inches in length, with a maximum of 10.9 inches – fine brookies by my personal standards.

Decades ago, at least for us Chittenden County folk, "South America Pond" was often cited by anglers as the most remote trout pond in the state. While not true, the spirit is very much on the mark, because it's a long hard drive to get to the trailhead, wherever you are coming from.

To access South America Pond, follow its namesake road north, from where it crosses Madison Brook, about three miles to a gravel pit at N 44.7101 W 71.7469.

A nice casting perch at South America Pond

The unsigned "road" that heads south to the pond is about fifty feet to the east, on the south side of South America Pond Road. It's a very rough road, wet and muddy in places. It's just a quarter mile walk, with a mild uphill trend, that leads into the pond's camps. You are better off just walking in for what is involved. The trail hits the shore before you reach a camp. On the right there is a fire ring, and flat ground where people have camped.

A rare spot for casting a long line with a fly is at these coordinates: N 44.7072 W 71.7430

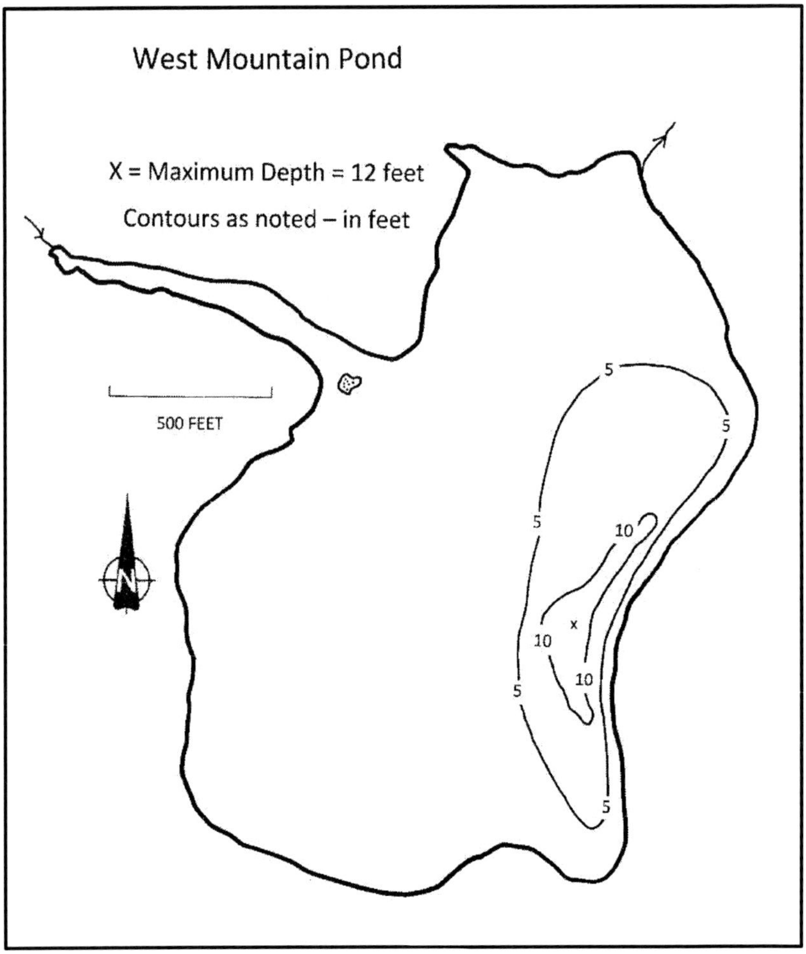
West Mountain Pond
X = Maximum Depth = 12 feet
Contours as noted – in feet
500 FEET
N
5
5
5
5
5
10
10
10
x

Unknown Pond

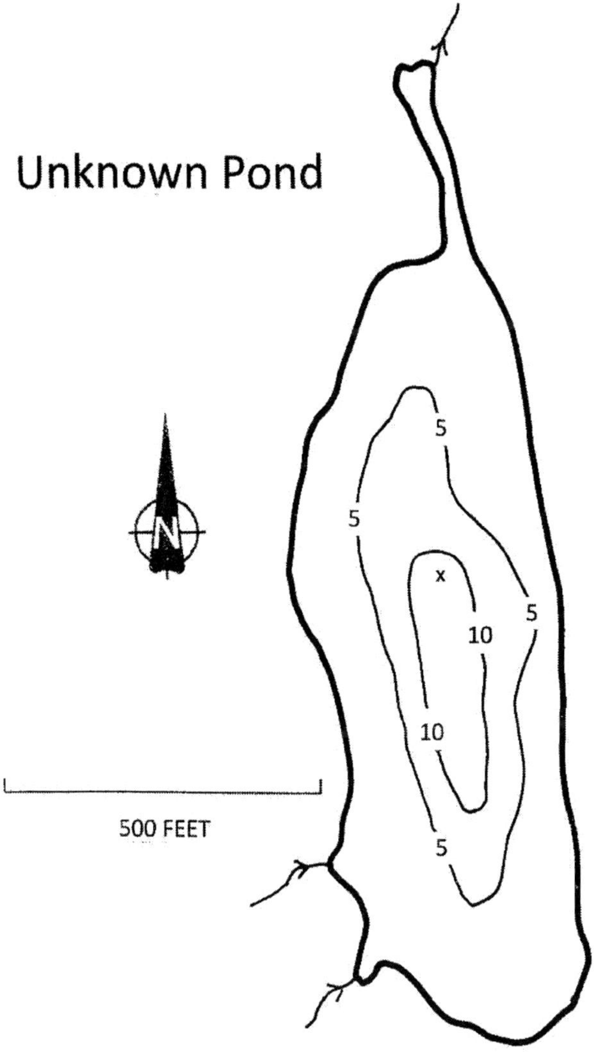

X = Maximum Depth = 13 feet

Contours as noted – in feet

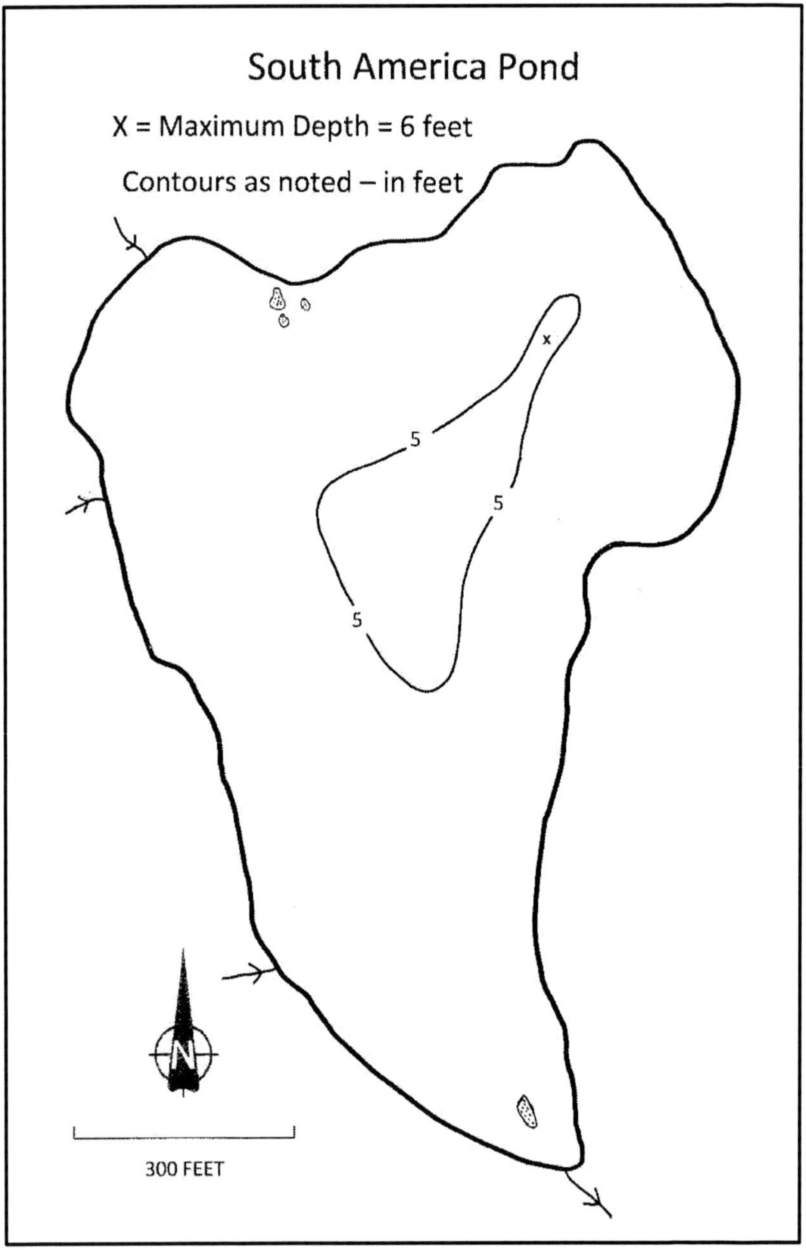
South America Pond
X = Maximum Depth = 6 feet
Contours as noted – in feet
x
5
5
5
N
300 FEET

Notes

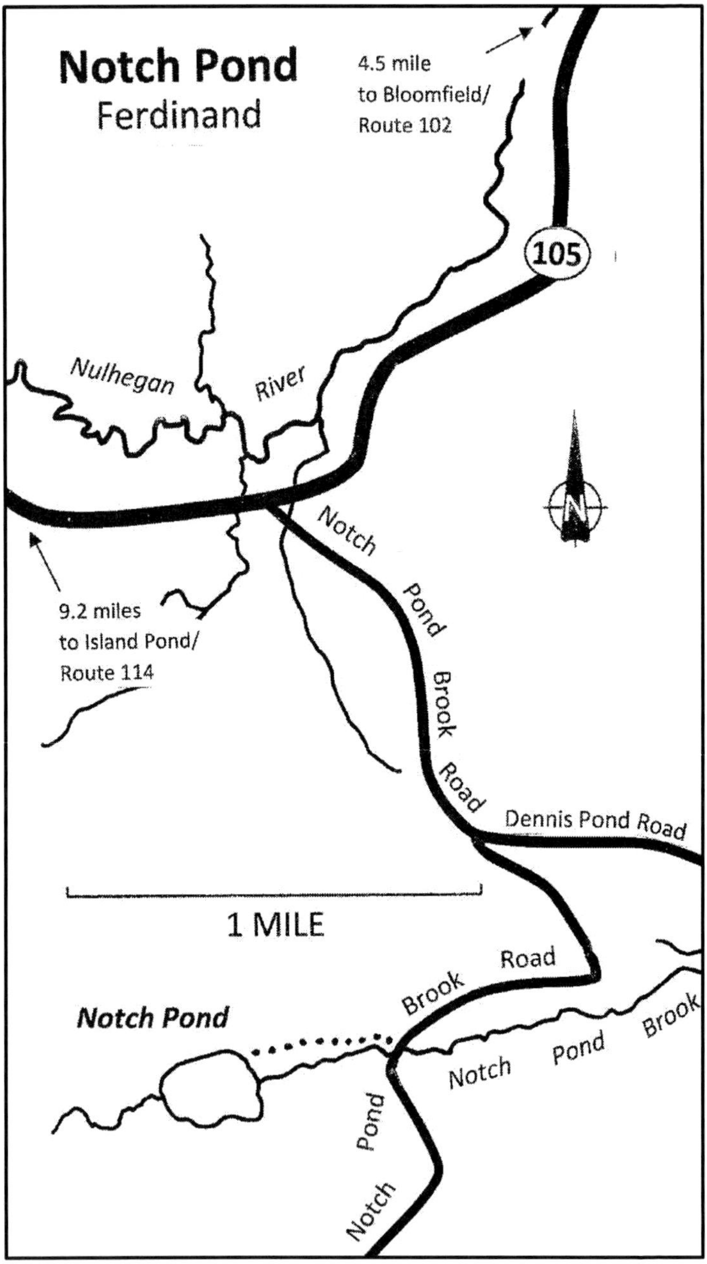
Notch Pond
Ferdinand
4.5 mile
to Bloomfield/
Route 102
105
Nulhegan
River
Notch
Pond
Brook
Road
9.2 miles
to Island Pond/
Route 114
Dennis Pond Road
1 MILE
Road
Brook
Notch Pond
Notch
Pond
Brook
Pond
Notch
N

Notch Pond, N 44.7387 W 71.7179

Notch Pond is in the town of Ferdinand. It is 22 acres in extent, and 30 feet deep at its maximum. It sits at an elevation of 1,596 feet. This is a sweet little pond, with a wonderful view of neighboring mountains without a whiff of human impact. Lush green in the late spring and summer, a riot of color in the fall, it is among the most scenic of our backwoods ponds.

The Seneca Mountain Range from Notch Pond

The trout here are doing really well. In 2011, the sampled trout were 94% stocked, averaging 11.3 inches, with a maximum length of 15 inches. Usually 1,000 fall fingerlings are stocked annually.

The easiest way into Notch Pond is from State Route 105 in Brunswick. From here take the Notch Pond Road south, bearing right at the first fork, and drive approximately two miles uphill to the Notch Pond trailhead, at these coordinates: N 44.7417 W 71.7091. From here it is less than a half mile to the pond, but it is decidedly uphill. About three quarters of the way there is a trail that forks to the right. Staying straight (left) is the shortest route to the pond and will land you at the "Notch Hilton."

The "Hilton" camp has a short dock. This, along with the cleared area in front of the camp are the best places you'll find for that long backcast. Again, ask permission if the owner is present. If the owner is absent, observe no-trace casting…no harm done.

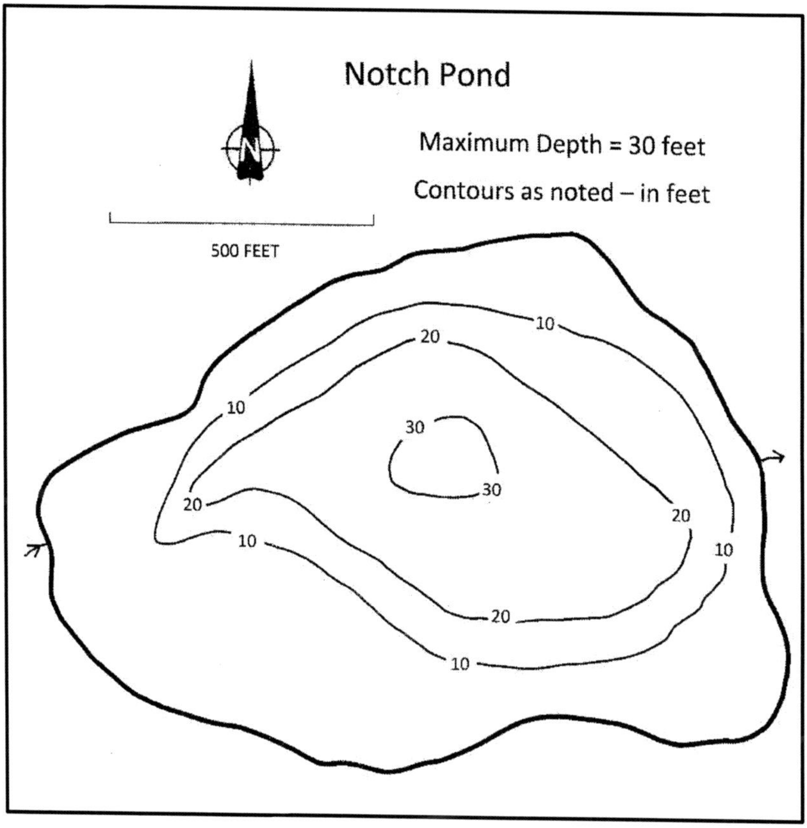
Notch Pond
Maximum Depth = 30 feet
Contours as noted – in feet
500 FEET
N
10
20
10
30
30
20
20
10
10
20
10
10

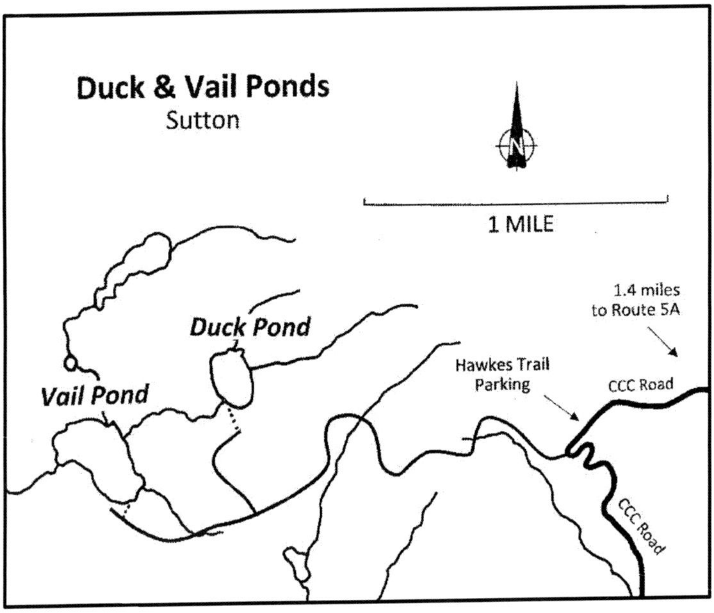
Duck & Vail Ponds
Sutton
N
1 MILE
1.4 miles
to Route 5A
Duck Pond
Vail Pond
Hawkes Trail
Parking
CCC Road
CCC Road

Duck and Vail Ponds

The area southwest of Lake Willoughby and Mt. Hor has several ponds. The two included here qualify as hike-ins even though the hikes are short. From the west, some of the roads have been decommissioned, which precludes their use. They still can be accessed from Route 5 via Dolloff Pond and CCC Roads, but the drive is longer and the road conditions are not as good as the access from Route 5A, which I recommend.

Duck Pond, N 44.7074 W 72.0660

Duck Pond is only an 8-acre pond, but has a surprising maximum depth of 43 feet. Its elevation is 1,700 feet. This pond sees an annual stocking of about 100 brook trout. In the most recent stocking these have been 10-inch trout. (In 2020, no trout were stocked.) The pond is on state land, but there is no developed boat access.

By backwoods-pond standards, there is a relatively large meadow on the south shore of the lake, which offers those of us who throw flies around a great place to cast, but not a place to camp. Primitive camping is allowed in the Willoughby State Forest, although it is not permitted this close to the lake (see pages 18-19.) There is an often-used campsite about 600 feet from the lake, beyond which vehicles cannot drive. This meets at least some of the state's criteria, but the requirement to camp at least 1,000 feet from a traveled road is questionable. Is this a traveled road? Well, it is at least the dead end of a traveled road. In my most recent experience, during high summer, I saw not a single car, once I was past the Herbert Hawkes Trailhead, a popular route up Mt. Hor. I had spent hours of road walking and driving.

The CCC Road, which accesses this area, is found about a third of a mile south of Lake Willoughby, on the west side of Route 5A. Take this road about two miles into the mountains. About a quarter mile past the Herbert Hawkes Trailhead, make a right turn onto another road at N 44.7076 W 72.0509. Continue on this road for nearly an additional mile, where yet another road to the right, at N 44.7038 W 72.0640, will take you to Duck Pond. (Continuing straight will lead you to Vail Pond.) From here it is a quarter-mile drive to a point where large rocks have been placed to exclude vehicles from traveling the last 600 feet to the pond, and that exceptional meadow.

Vail Pond, N 44.7049 W 72.0722

Vail Pond, in Sutton, has 16 acres at an elevation of 1,491 feet. It has the same maximum depth as its neighbor Duck Pond, at 43 feet. Here is a rare backwoods pond that is stocked with rainbows, not brookies. Recently, these fish have run 10 inches or better in size. Usually about 200 of these rainbows are dropped in.

The state boat access is undeveloped. It is appropriate for smaller boats.

“Meadows” are rare in remote ponds; this is at Duck Pond

To reach Vail Pond simply, see above, and do not take the road to the right that leads to Duck. Just continue straight, for another half mile. (A road to the left goes to Marl Pond.) The road you are on ends at a private camp. Two or three hundred feet before you get to the camp, there is a very narrow, rough road that only a true redneck would drive on. It's on the right, and it's only a few hundred feet to the pond. Enough said.

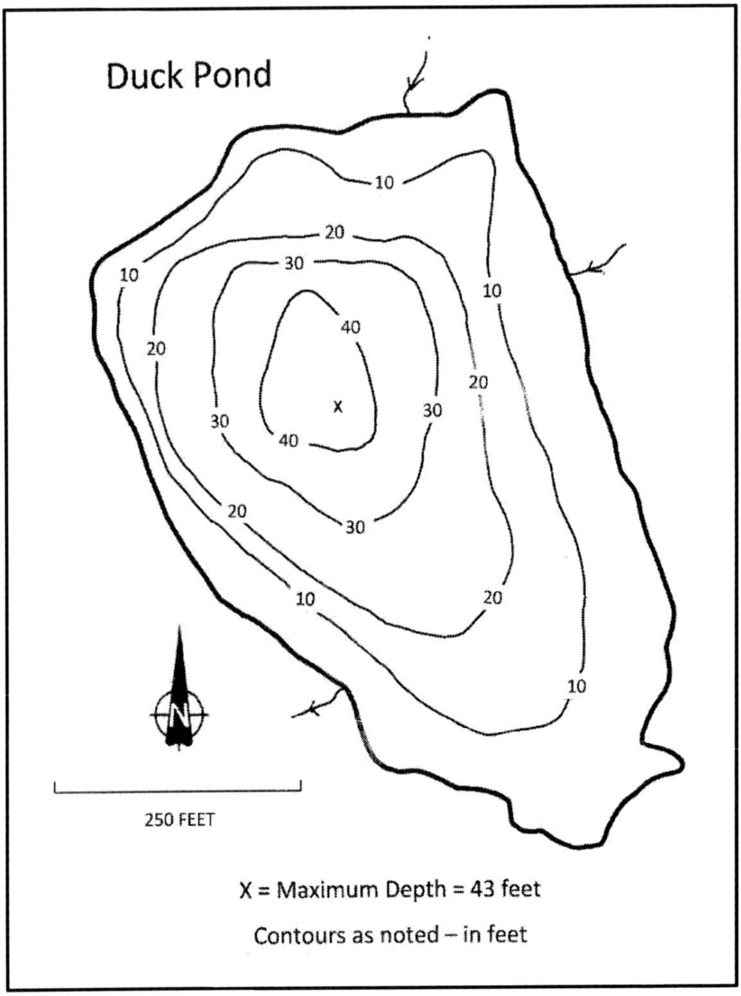
Duck Pond
10
20
30
40
X
N
250 FEET
X = Maximum Depth = 43 feet
Contours as noted – in feet

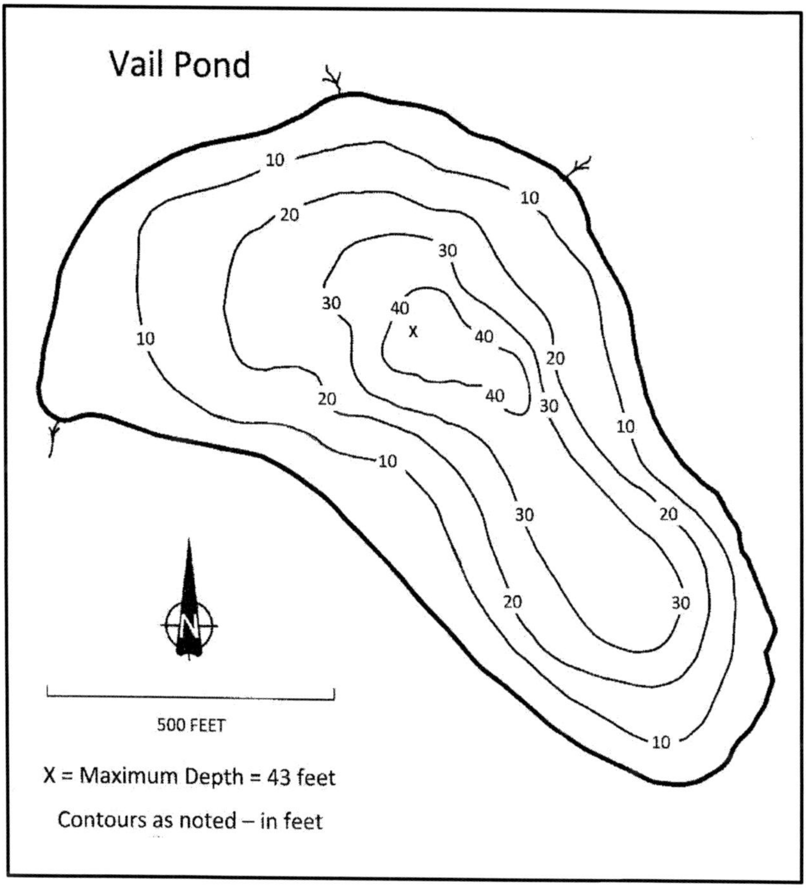
Vail Pond
10
20
30
40
X
500 FEET
X = Maximum Depth = 43 feet
Contours as noted – in feet

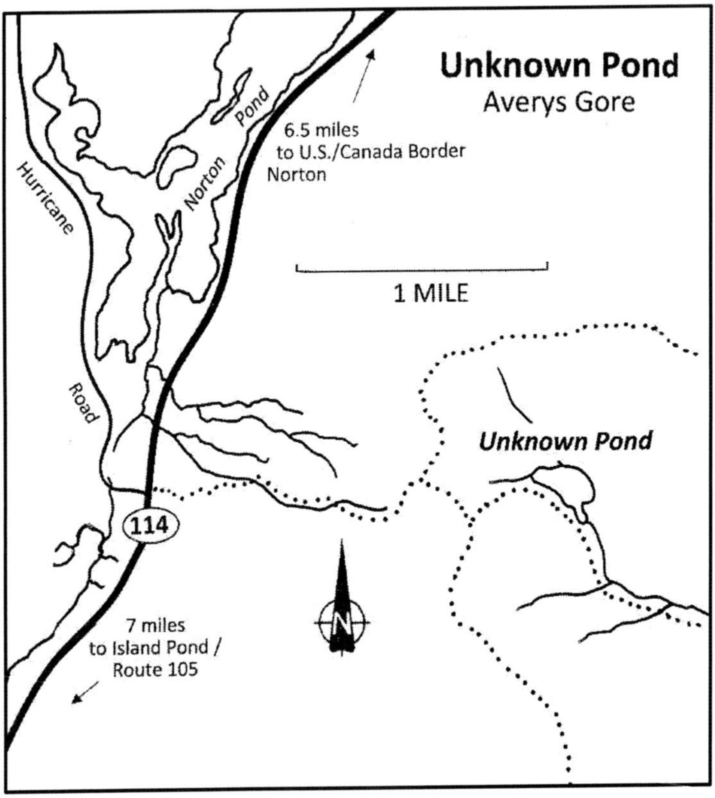
Unknown Pond
Averys Gore
Pond
Norton
Hurricane
Road
6.5 miles
to U.S./Canada Border
Norton
1 MILE
Unknown Pond
114
7 miles
to Island Pond /
Route 105
N

Unknown Pond, N 44.9105 W 71.8436

One of two "Unknown" ponds in the state, this one is in Averys Gore. It has 19 acres and a maximum depth of 14 feet. Its elevation is 2,319 feet. This Northeast Kingdom pond was last stocked in 2009. The following year the pond was sampled, and 95% of the trout found were wild, and had an average size that approached 10 inches. That's a siren call for me. In the last few years there has been considerable trail development, including a trail network that connects several mountain tops – Bluff, Middle, and Gore Mountains. It starts in Island Pond and runs to the northern end of Norton Pond.

The trailhead to what is now called the Unknown Pond Trail is located on the east side of State Route 114, about 75 feet north of where Hurricane Road comes in on the west. A good pair of legs is required for this trip. In less than a mile and a half, you climb almost one thousand feet to this trail's juncture with the Middle Mountain and Bluff Mountain Trails. From here you head south (right) on the Bluff Mountain Trail, for about a half mile, where the Gore "Road" comes in on the left. Take this left another half mile to the pond; the Bluff Mountain Trail continues straight south.

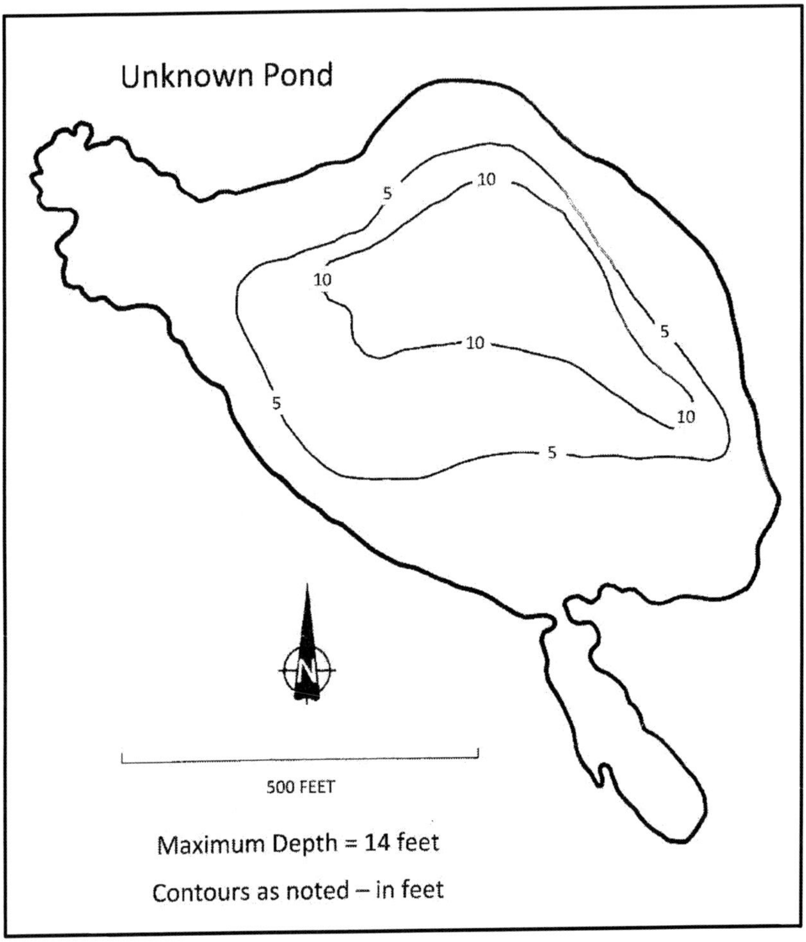
Unknown Pond
5
10
10
10
5
5
10
5
500 FEET
Maximum Depth = 14 feet
Contours as noted – in feet

PLEASE JOIN A CHAPTER !

Vermont Chapters of Trout Unlimited

(Currently active)

Trout Unlimited Vermont Council
1719 Route 100B
Moretown, VT 05660
Tel # 802-496-7971, https://www.vttucouncil.org

Southwestern Vermont Chapter #049
Trout Unlimited – Southwestern Vermont, Chapter #049
PO Box 88
Manchester, Vermont 05254
tuswvt@gmail.com; Facebook: @TUSWVT;
https://tusouthwesternvermont.org

Central Vermont Trout Unlimited, Chapter #138
Central Vermont Trout Unlimited
522 Harbor View Dr.
Saint Albans, VT 05478
https://vttu.org

Greater Upper Valley Trout Unlimited, Chapter #226
https://greateruppervalley.tu.org/greateruppervalley/guvtu-board-members

Connecticut River Valley Trout Unlimited, Chapter #450
Chris Campany, Vice President
chriscampany123@gmail.com; (802) 257-4547;
http://tuconnriver.weebly.com

Mad Dog Trout Unlimited, Chapter #539
All Correspondence addressed to:
PO Box 892
Montpelier VT 05601
http://www.maddogtu.org

Useful Contacts

Vermont Fish & Wildlife Department
1 National Life Drive, Davis 2
Montpelier, VT 05602-3702
802-828-1000
fwinformation@vermont.gov
www.vtfishandwildlife.com

Green Mountain National Forest
231 North Main Street
Rutland, VT 05701
802-747-6700
Rochester Ranger Station – 802-767-4261
Manchester Ranger Station – 802-362-2307

Vermont Department of Forests, Parks and Recreation
1 National Life Drive, Davis 2
Montpelier, VT 05602-3801
https://fpr.vermont.gov/contact_us
https://fpr.vermont.gov

PLEASE JOIN !
Green Mountain Club
4711 Waterbury-Stowe Road
Waterbury Center, Vermont 05677
802.244.7037
gmc@greenmountainclub.org
www.greenmountainclub.org

Sources and Resources

Agency of Natural Resources, Department of Environmental Conservation; (depth charts)
https://dec.vermont.gov/watershed/lakes-ponds/data-maps/charts

ANR – Atlas Lite, Vermont Agency of Natural Resources, Department of Environmental Conservation 2020;
https://anrmaps.vermont.gov/websites/anra5Lite

Day Hiker's Guide to Vermont: Exploring the Green Mountain State, 6th Edition, The Green Mountain Club, 2011
www.greenmountainclub.org

Long Trail Guide (28th Edition),
The Green Mountain Club, 2017
www.greenmountainclub.org

The New Atlas of Vermont Trout Ponds: A GPS Compatible Guidebook, Peter Shea, Wind Knot Publishing, 2018
www.windknotpublishing.com

Vermont Lakes in Depth, Northern Cartographic, 1981

Vermont Fish & Wildlife Department
Agency of Natural Resources (stocking)
https://anrweb.vt.gov/FWD/FW/FishStockingSearch.aspx

Vermont Fish & Wildlife Department, Agency of Natural Resources (water access)
https://anrweb.vt.gov/FWD/FW/FishingAccessAreas.aspx

Other Maps Sources: Google Earth®, Google Maps®, GAIA®

Index

map(s), text